W0082521

National Defense Research Institute

# Taiwan's National Security, Defense Policy, and Weapons Procurement Processes

MICHAEL D. SWAINE

Prepared for the
Office of the Secretary of Defense

## RAND

This report examines Taiwan's national security decisionmaking structure and process and the primary factors guiding its defense strategy, force structure, and military procurement decisions. The analysis attempts to explain the motives and interests determining Taiwan's national security policy and defense plans and its decisions to acquire major weapons and related support systems from foreign sources, especially the United States.

This study was conducted as part of a project on "Taiwan's Evolving Views of Deterrence and National Defense: Implications for U.S. Policy." It was conducted for OUSDP/ISA (Asia-Pacific Office) within RAND's National Defense Research Institute; a federally funded research and development center sponsored by the Office of the Secretary of Defense, the Joint Staff, the unified commands, and the defense agencies.

# CONTENTS

# FIGURES

The Republic of China (ROC) government has no formal, institutionalized and regularized interagency process or mechanism for national security strategy formulation and implementation.[1] Taiwan's national security strategy (including its national strategic objectives and the major principles guiding its foreign and defense policies) is developed in a fragmentary way, within responsible agencies, or by the president alone, through largely separate, and often private, interactions with senior civilian and military officials.

Below the president, the most important senior officials and advisors influencing overall national security policy (including foreign policy) are the National Security Council (NSC) secretary-general, the foreign minister, the defense minister and, to a lesser extent, the premier. No influential inner circle of formal or informal national security advisors to the president exists within the ROC government. The Taiwan NSC as a body does not have the authority and influence of its U.S. counterpart. However, efforts aimed in part at strengthening the role of the ROC National Security Council might increase its influence and thereby regularize somewhat the overall national security policy process.

ROC President Lee Teng-hui's attention and expertise in the broad national security policy realm are primarily focused on nonmilitary issues, especially the major features of Taiwan's multipronged effort to increase its international political and diplomatic profile and the

---

[1] In this report, the terms "Taiwan" and "Republic of China" are used interchangeably.

general contours of Taiwan's increasing interactions with Mainland China.

Most informed observers believe that Lee Teng-hui wants to attain some level of international acceptance of Taiwan as an equal, separate, and sovereign entity, both to consolidate his domestic political base and historical legacy and to provide Taiwan with greater leverage in a future negotiation for the establishment of a loose confederation-type relationship with Beijing.

Taiwan's defense policy and procurement decisionmaking processes are centered on the professional military. Its defense strategy and force structure are primarily determined by the ROC General Staff Headquarters (GSH), within the broad parameters provided by Taiwan's overall national security policy, and with critical inputs provided by the three service headquarters. An increasingly important policy organ within the GSH is the recently established Office of Defense and Strategic Studies (ODSS). The level of influence over defense policy and procurement decisions exerted by senior civilian officials can vary significantly, depending upon the personal influence of the individual holding the office. Taiwan's current highly competent and activist defense minister, Tang Fei, is reportedly increasing the influence of the Ministry of National Defense (MND) over both decisionmaking arenas.

A National Military Council (*guofang junshi huiyi*) (NMC) has been proposed as a mechanism for bringing together the key members of Taiwan's national security and defense leaderships to advise the president, make critical decisions, and strengthen policy coordination between the defense and foreign affairs policy realms. However, the effectiveness of the NMC would depend almost entirely upon the president's willingness to use the forum and the information and analysis provided by subordinate defense organs (the NMC would not possess its own staff).

President Lee Teng-hui is clearly committed to the maintenance of an effective military. However, it is unclear whether he supports a strong military primarily for *political* purposes, as part of a larger strategy toward Beijing and Washington, or primarily for genuine *warfighting* purposes, to deter or defeat a possible attack from the Mainland. Each viewpoint suggests a different presidential approach to force modernization and procurement. Many observers suspect that Lee adheres to the former viewpoint. Hence, they are particularly concerned that Lee underestimates the military danger posed by China and overestimates the ability and willingness of the United States to come to Taiwan's assistance in the early stages of a conflict.

Regardless of his defense views, Lee Teng-hui apparently does not play a very active role in either oversight or decisionmaking regarding either the general features or the specific contents of Taiwan's defense policy or force structure. He reportedly does not regularly and systematically supervise or intervene in shaping defense policy; nor does he seek to actively coordinate and integrate, either conceptually or operationally, the defense and foreign policy arenas.

Lee Teng-hui reportedly relies primarily on former Chief of the General Staff (CGS) (now Ministry of National Defense, MND) General Tang Fei for advice on defense policy and procurement issues, the general handling of the military, and relations with the Legislative Yuan concerning military issues. Lee most likely promoted Tang to the MND leadership post because of the latter's high competence, especially in the areas of defense strategy, military modernization, and military restructuring, and because of his apparent sensitivity to both the larger political environment on Taiwan and to the complex Taiwan-U.S.-PRC relationship.

The GSH serves as the coordinating body and operational locus for the defense strategy/force structure and budgetary/procurement processes within Taiwan's defense policy arena. The CGS is by far the most powerful and influential figure within the GSH. Despite its formal role as a broad coordination and supervision mechanism for the armed services, the GSH in reality serves as a staff agency for the CGS. Thus, the character, personal relations, and service orientation of the CGS exert a significant, sometimes decisive, influence over the operations and outlook of the GSH.

Because it does not contain the most-senior leaders of each armed service, the GSH cannot effectively and authoritatively coordinate the activities of the individual services. Hence, the existence of the GSH as a separate leading bureaucratic entity from the armed services presents a potential obstacle to the establishment of true joint-ness among the three services.

Closer media and Legislative Yuan (LY) scrutiny of the military has (1) contributed to broader efforts by the LY to reduce defense spending in specific areas, (2) greatly extended the time required to complete the procurement process, (3) led to greater efforts by the MND to strengthen its role as an intermediary between the LY and the military, and (4) contributed greatly to an effort to place the GSH (and hence the CGS) entirely under the MND.

Taiwan's defense strategy defines three key missions for the ROC armed forces, listed in general order of priority: (1) air superiority (*zhikong*), (2) sea denial (*zhihai*), and (3) antilanding warfare (*fandenglu*). The ROC Air Force's air superiority mission primarily emphasizes air-to-air interception. The ROC Navy's sea denial mission focuses almost exclusively on countering various forms of Chinese naval blockades. The ROC Army's antilanding warfare mission is primarily directed toward countering paratroop attacks, followed by a large-scale amphibious assault on Taiwan.

Taiwan's defense strategy is not based upon a concept of joint warfighting, because of the small size of its military, the limited expanse of the battlespaces involved, the limited technical capabilities of its weapons systems, and the purely defensive nature of the mission given to each service. Its strategy also reflects the severe restrictions on operational capabilities imposed by its relatively small defense budget and the larger "stovepiped" nature of the ROC military structure.

Officially, the concepts of "resolute defense" and "effective deterrence" basic to the ROC defense strategy suggest that Taiwan must acquire the capability to carry out the above three military missions successfully without outside assistance. In reality, ROC defense planners realize that Taiwan is almost certainly incapable of effectively resisting an all-out and prolonged attack from the PRC without help from the United States. Therefore, Taiwan's defense strategy is primarily designed, on the operational level, to hold out and give the United States time to intervene. However, Taipei hopes that Beijing will hesitate to initiate an attack, fearing possible significant initial losses, even if confident of eventually prevailing with its numerically superior overall force.

The ROC military's primary mission suggests an array of current and future equipment needs, from more-sophisticated and integrated C3I and reconnaissance and early warning systems, to more-advanced surface combatants, more-advanced air-to-air and air-to-surface missiles, submarines, improved antisubmarine warfare (ASW) platforms, including more-modern air ASW aircraft, and more-capable countermeasures against ballistic and cruise missiles. The ROC military will also need to undertake a costly streamlining, restructuring, reeducating, and retraining of its administrative and combat units to create the kind of force that can meet the Chinese threat over the long term.

Despite such a considerable array of hardware and software service needs, budgetary and manpower limitations, technical constraints, leadership preferences, and the hesitancy of most foreign suppliers to provide specific weapons systems place significant limits on what and how much Taiwan can acquire, especially over the near to medium term.

Those GSH offices exercising the greatest influence over planning and procurement decisions are J-5 (planning) and, to a lesser extent, J-4 (logistics). The former takes primary responsibility for drawing up the military-wide defense plan, through input provided by the individual services and the other J-5 offices. It also takes the lead in formulating military-wide procurement decisions, based upon the planning and related force structure conclusions and procurement proposals developed under its supervision. The J-4 is primarily responsible for implementing acquisition decisions.

The defense plans submitted by the services must generally adhere to the specific mission of each service. Long-term (usually ten-year) defense and budget plans normally provide basic guidance for five-year and annual plans. Annual force structure and budget plans generally roll over from year to year on the basis of these longer-term plans and hence contain few major changes. However, both plans can sometimes fluctuate significantly, primarily because of changes in the perceived threat posed by the Mainland, the changing preferences of key decisionmakers such as the CGS, and the opportunities presented by the sudden availability of previously unobtainable foreign weapons.

As part of his extensive influence over the operations of the GSH, the CGS has the authority to shape and alter defense plans and budget distributions to the individual services. However, such influence consists primarily of shifts in the relative emphasis placed upon the forces or finances of a particular service, not wholesale transformations that contravene the parameters set by long-term defense and budget plans.

GSH assessments of service procurement requests are based primarily on the perceived relevancy of each request to Taiwan's overall defense strategy/force modernization plan and its likely cost within the estimated defense budget for that year. The latter evaluation is generally guided by a desire to avoid items that take up significant portions of the entire annual defense budget, unless they are specifically (and strongly) favored by the CGS. The former evaluation determines the relevancy of each service's request to its core defense mission.

The ROC Air Force will almost always stress the acquisition of capabilities directly relating to air-to-air interception, the Navy will almost always stress the acquisition of antishipping capabilities, and the Army will almost always stress the acquisition of equipment to oppose a direct ground-based assault against Taiwan's main island.

Formal proposals for procurement items, whether determined by the GSH/J-5-led procurement committee or the individual services, must be submitted to the CGS. The CGS evaluates these proposals and can make changes before they are finalized and then submitted to the MND. The CGS can, and often does, press to obtain disproportionately high procurement orders for systems needed by his particular service. However, each CGS must be attentive to the overall force structure requirements contained in the ROC's five- and ten-year defense plans.

The MND normally does not have the expertise to evaluate or challenge specific procurement requests. However, the newly named defense minister, Tang Fei, as an experienced former senior military officer, will doubtless query individual requests and could exert a greater influence over the overall procurement process. In fact, there is some evidence that he is pushing for a more comprehensive and rational planning, programming, and budgeting process, to be housed in part within the MND.

President Lee Teng-hui lacks the expertise to evaluate the technical or operational value or necessity of a requested defense-related system. He usually relies on the views of the defense minister and the CGS. Yet he sometimes seeks, during meetings of the GSH procurement committee, to ensure the inclusion of one or two high-profile weapons systems at the expense of other less prominent but equally important systems. This is allegedly done because Lee Teng-hui views weaponry more as symbols of reassurance and resolve than as key components of a larger force structure designed to attain genuine warfighting objectives, and because he values U.S.-supplied weapons systems in particular as critical indicators of greater U.S. support for Taiwan.

However, Lee Teng-hui's influence on the procurement process is highly sporadic and usually exerted in support of weapons systems that were already under serious consideration by the professional military on the basis of their merit as components of existing force structure modernization plans. No interviewee stated that presidential intervention has resulted in the inclusion of weapons systems that were strongly opposed by the majority of the senior military leadership. Indeed, some interviewees insist that the professional military is able to resist efforts by any civilian ROC official, including the president, to insert major procurement items into the budget contrary to their wishes.

Despite serious and sensational procurement scandals in the early 1990s, and the development of significant reform proposals, no formal, systematic process of legislative examination or supervision of the procurement process currently exists. In general, scrutiny of procurement proposals by the Legislative Yuan is sporadic and largely nontechnical in nature, given its limited expertise on defense matters and its lack of access to the early stages of the procurement decisionmaking process. The LY can request a hearing or a report on specific procurement items that it discovers or that are brought to its attention. Yet the dominant influence over defense matters exerted by conservative Kuomintang (KMT) members of the LY National Defense Committee continues to prevent substantive changes in the procurement proposals prepared by the military and approved by the president and the Executive Yuan.

Although increasing significantly during the mid 1990s, the level of LY influence over defense matters reportedly declined somewhat by the end of the decade. This has resulted primarily from (a) the continued failure of Democratic Progressive Party (DPP) and other opposition political parties to develop significant defense-related expertise, (b) the lowering of concerns among opposition political leaders about the political influence exerted over the military by conservative KMT members, and (c) the gradual convergence of views on defense matters between mainstream KMT and mainstream DPP politicians. However, the ability of the LY to oversee military affairs, including defense and national security strategies, could increase significantly in the future once a proposed streamlining of Taiwan's military authority system goes into effect. Under these reforms, not only will the LY be able to examine military views and decisions more closely, but it will also likely have the authority to evaluate defense budget and procurement issues *before* critical decisions are made, and thereby more extensively shape the size and composition of the defense budget.

Several ROC observers remarked that the U.S. Congress and U.S. defense industry corporations also play a significant role in Taiwan's procurement decisionmaking process. Many U.S. Congresspersons have a very strong interest in Taiwan security issues, for both national security and pro-democracy reasons, and in response to the narrower political and economic interests of their constituencies. In addition, many U.S. defense industries have an obvious interest in expanding their level of business with Taiwan through increased U.S. military sales to the island. As a result, U.S. political representatives and businesses will often take an active interest in the type and origin of various weapons systems available to Taiwan and will at times express their preferences regarding such systems to ROC officials, including both high- and low-level individuals responsible for defense policy and procurement issues. This is particularly true of U.S. businesses that have very active representative offices in Taipei and thus have much easier, and more direct, access to ROC defense officials. This type of informal and indirect U.S. involvement has frequently influenced the procurement process, according to knowledgeable observers.

The above research findings pose a few implications for the U.S. defense relationship with Taiwan, especially regarding the sale of military equipment.

First, the United States should continue to strengthen and expand its defense-related contacts with the ROC both to assist the ROC in rationalizing its defense planning and budgeting process and to more accurately assess Taiwan's requests for military sales from and cooperation with the United States. These contacts should include strategic dialogues, and advice and assistance designed to improve equipment training, procurement and acquisition processes, and management techniques. At the same time, the United States should exercise utmost caution with respect to interactions with the ROC that might be construed as aimed at the establishment of joint operational capabilities (i.e., so-called interoperability) between ROC and U.S. combat forces.

Second, the United States should strive to develop and maintain close contacts with and knowledge about Taiwan's key national security and defense decisionmakers, especially the president, minister cf defense, NSC secretary-general, and chief of the general staff.

Third, the United States should be aware that a variety of motives could lie behind each of Taiwan's requests for major weapons systems and types of security assistance and that some systems and operating personnel might not receive adequate training and support services. Attempts should be made to identify and disentangle military from possible nonmilitary motives and to realistically assess (and convey to the ROC) what is required to deploy and maintain a particular major weapons system. The United States should also work with the ROC to reduce the influence of parochial U.S. political and business interests on ROC arms purchase requests.

# ACKNOWLEDGMENTS

This report covers a subject that is rarely treated in either the open or classified literature concerning Taiwan. Hence, the descriptions and analyses presented herein rely greatly on information obtained through interviews with many senior Taiwan civilian and military leaders, officials, scholars, journalists, and very knowledgeable U.S. observers of Taiwan defense matters. I owe a great debt of gratitude to each of these individuals for their willingness to discuss, in a frank and open manner, such a sensitive topic, and for their excellent insights. These individuals requested that their names not be cited in this report.

The report was formally reviewed by Dr. Paul Godwin, consultant on Chinese security issues and retired professor at the National War College and Mr. Eric McVadon, consultant on Chinese and Taiwan security issues and retired Rear Admiral, U.S. Navy. The incorporation of their excellent comments and suggestions has greatly improved the overall quality of the report. Valuable informal written comments on various drafts were provided by Andrew Yang, Alexander Huang, and Jean-Pierre Cabestan. My secretary, Madeline Taylor, pulled together the final version of the manuscript and provided all manner of logistical support. Joan Myers assisted in compiling the organizational charts and Patricia Bedrosian contributed her excellent editorial expertise.

In the final analysis, however, the information, judgments, and assessments contained in this report are entirely my responsibility.

| | |
|---|---|
| ASW | Antisubmarine Warfare |
| C3I | Command, Control, Communications, and Intelligence |
| CBM | Confidence-Building Measure |
| CCK | Chiang Ch'ing-kuo |
| CGS | Chief of the General Staff |
| CinC | Commander-in-Chief |
| CIS | Commonwealth of Independent States |
| DCGS | Deputy Chief of the General Staff |
| DPP | Democratic Progressive Party |
| EW | Early Warning |
| EY | Executive Yuan |
| GSH | General Staff Headquarters |
| INPR | Institute for National Policy Research |
| IW | Information Warfare |
| KMT | Kuomintang (Nationalist) Party |
| LY | Legislative Yuan |
| MAC | Mainland Affairs Council |

| | |
|---|---|
| MND | Ministry of National Defense |
| MoFA | Ministry of Foreign Affairs |
| NCO | Noncommissioned Officer |
| NMC | National Military Council |
| NSB | National Security Bureau |
| NSC | National Security Council |
| NUC | National Unification Council |
| NURC | National Unification Research Council |
| ODSS | Office of Defense and Strategic Studies |
| PLA | People's Liberation Army |
| PPBS | Planning, Programming, and Budgeting System |
| PRC | People's Republic of China |
| RMA | Revolution in Military Affairs |
| ROC | Republic of China |
| SAC | Strategy Advisory Committee |
| TMD | Theater Missile Defense |
| VCGS | Vice Chief of the General Staff |

# Chapter One

# INTRODUCTION

Since the early 1990s, U.S. policy toward the Republic of China (ROC, also referred to in this study as Taiwan), including its arms sale policy, has assumed an increasingly important role in overall U.S. policy calculations and concerns in the Asia-Pacific region. This is primarily because political and military tensions between Taiwan and the People's Republic of China (PRC) have increased dramatically during the decade, posing serious implications for the U.S. commitment to a peaceful, mutually agreed upon resolution of the long-standing dispute between Taipei and Beijing, as well as its commitment to provide Taiwan with military assistance to maintain its self-defense capabilities.

This increasingly serious situation has emerged for several closely interrelated reasons. Since at least the mid 1990s, the PRC has sought to deter what it perceives as Taiwan's "search for independence" by (a) engaging in military displays designed in part to intimidate the Taiwan population, and (b) generally increasing the credibility of the Chinese threat of force through the acquisition of potent weapons systems able to support a variety of armed actions against the ROC.[1] Beijing has also attempted to pressure the United States to reduce its military assistance to the ROC, allegedly to reduce

---

[1] China's ability to increase its military pressure against Taiwan has grown significantly during the decade because of sustained high Chinese economic growth rates, which have resulted in budgets large enough to allow selective modernization of elements of the PLA, despite the low priority assigned to that task by Beijing. Much of the PLA modernization has been focused on coping with Taiwan, either matching capabilities acquired by Taiwan or developing systems specifically for potential use against Taiwan—such as short-range ballistic missiles with conventional warheads.

Taiwan's willingness to seek independence and to induce it to enter into reunification talks with the Mainland. These PRC actions have prompted the ROC to request that the United States provide larger amounts of more potent weapons and related support systems to Taiwan, to maintain Taiwan's ability to counter growing PRC military pressure and thereby remain free from political coercion, and to deter a PRC attack. In response to these developments, the U.S. Congress has become increasingly concerned as to whether the current level and quality of U.S. military sales to Taiwan, provided for under the Taiwan Relations Act, are sufficient to maintain the security of the ROC. In addition, some U.S. policymakers have begun to ask whether U.S. forces should establish some level of operational coordination and cooperation with their ROC counterparts. The latter issue has received increasing attention as a result of the growing debate over possible Taiwanese involvement in a U.S.-led East Asian theater missile defense (TMD) system. Beijing has asserted that the most intolerable aspect of TMD for Taiwan would be that it would imply a reestablishment of close operational links between U.S. and ROC military forces.

All of these developments have greatly increased the significance of U.S. arms sales and military assistance to Taiwan as a potential source of instability in the overall Sino-U.S. relationship; such instability could undermine the peace and stability of the entire East Asian region. These potential dangers highlight the importance of U.S. efforts to, on the one hand, help Taipei improve its defense planning and budgeting process and, on the other hand, more accurately assess Taiwan's requests for both increased military sales from and enhanced military cooperation with the United States. Such U.S. efforts are necessary to effectively and realistically maintain Taiwan's ability to provide for its own defense, to avoid excessively provoking China to escalate its attempts to coerce Taiwan through military means, and to reassure the U.S. Congress that the United States is providing Taiwan with what it realistically needs to maintain its security.

The attainment of these objectives requires a clear understanding of the influence on Taiwan's arms purchase requests exerted by an array of ROC internal factors, including Taiwan's overall national security and defense policy objectives and priorities, the force requirements implied by Taiwan's defense strategy and threat assessments, the internal decisionmaking features of Taiwan's weapons procurement process, the influence of Taiwan's political calculations toward the United States, and the overall role played by senior leadership personalities and bureaucratic relationships.  By examining these internal factors, this study attempts to answer such questions as Which senior Taiwan leaders and institutions exert the greatest influence over national security and defense policy?  What level and type of influence do they exert?  What is Taiwan's defense strategy and how does it influence force structure and procurement priorities?  How does Taiwan's procurement process function?  To what extent are Taiwan's foreign weapons purchase decisions motivated by internal political or bureaucratic, as opposed to deterrence or warfighting, factors?

The analysis is divided into three chapters.  Chapter Two examines the major features of Taiwan's senior-level national security policymaking apparatus most relevant to foreign arms purchase decisions. This includes an analysis of the leaders and key civilian and military organizations that determine the general strategic principles and political guidelines shaping Taiwan's defense policy and general political relationship with critical providers of military equipment such as the United States.  An important aspect of this presentation is an assessment of the specific relationship between the ROC president and his senior national security advisors and officials and the views of the ROC president regarding the level and type of military threat posed by the People's Republic of China.  The chapter concludes with an overall assessment of the main features of Taiwan's national security decisionmaking process.

Chapter Three examines the workings of the Taiwan defense sector directly relevant to foreign arms purchase decisions.  It focuses on the main features and linkages between Taiwan's defense strategy, force structure, and procurement process.  As in Chapter Two, the analysis first examines the major organizations and leaders directly involved in critical decisionmaking in these three areas.  This includes a discussion of the policy roles played by individual senior military and civilian leaders, senior organs and departments of the Taiwan General Staff Headquarters, and the military services. This is followed by an overview of Taiwan's current defense strategy and its implications for force structure and procurement issues.  The chapter concludes with an overall assessment of the main elements of Taiwan's procurement decisionmaking process.

Chapter Four draws several overall conclusions of particular interest to U.S. policymakers and provides a few policy recommendations relevant to the defense relationship with Taiwan, including the sale of military equipment.

As indicated in the overall analysis, it is important to keep in mind that many aspects of Taiwan's national security, defense, and weapons procurement decisionmaking processes are in flux, as a result of major changes currently under way that directly or indirectly affect the institutional and procedural environments of the national security and defense sectors as a whole. We have tried to incorporate such changes into our analysis to the greatest extent possible. However, given the inevitable uncertainties presented by this changing environment, many of our conclusions must be considered tentative, subject to further changes, confirmation, or refutation by unfolding events.

The analysis presented in this report is based primarily upon confidential interviews with senior ROC civilian and military leaders, officials, scholars, journalists, and very knowledgeable U.S. observers of Taiwan's defense matters. These interviews were conducted by the author during trips taken to Washington, D.C., and Taipei, Taiwan, during summer 1996, summer 1997, January 1998, and May 1999.

# Chapter Two

# NATIONAL SECURITY POLICY

Taipei's decisions to acquire specific foreign weapons platforms and related support systems are significantly influenced by the overall priorities, interests, and decisionmaking features of Taiwan's senior-level national security policymaking apparatus. Senior leaders and organizations within this apparatus shape Taiwan's national strategic objectives and the strategic principles guiding Taiwan's foreign and defense policies, which in turn influence both the broad parameters of Taiwan's force structure and specific procurement decisions regarding weapons and related support systems.

## SENIOR ORGANIZATIONS AND LEADERS

The basic structure of Taiwan's national security policy apparatus is presented in Figure 1. This apparatus centers on the leaders of seven key institutions.

1. Offices of the President and Vice President

2. Office of the Premier of the Executive Yuan (EY)

3. National Security Council (NSC)

4. Ministry of Foreign Affairs (MoFA)

5. Ministry of National Defense (MND)

6. General Staff Headquarters (GSH)

7. National Security Bureau (NSB)

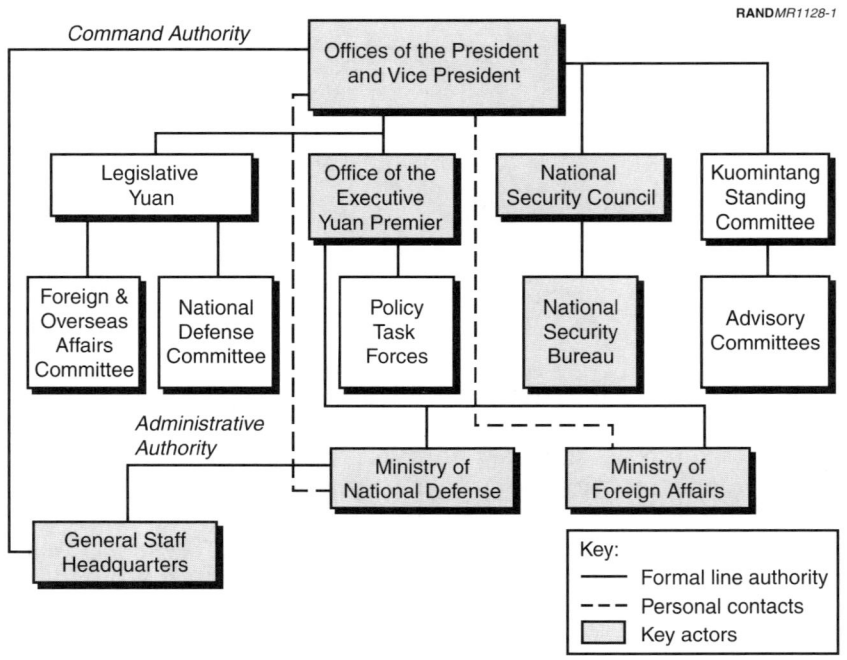

**Figure 1—ROC National Security Policy Apparatus**

This chapter will discuss the main features of each of these institutions and their leaders and then will summarize the overall national security decisionmaking process.

## Offices of the President and Vice President

The president of the Republic of China exercises supreme authority over national security policy at the level of grand strategy as well as over the broad contours of foreign and defense policy. As Taiwan's sole nationally elected head of state and as commander-in-chief of the ROC armed forces, the president has the final word on such basic national security issues as the formulation of national strategic objectives, the basic principles and concepts guiding foreign and defense policies, the general diplomatic and political strategy toward the People's Republic of China, and the direction of Taiwan's military in time of war.

Operationally, the president exercises control over senior, subordinate actors of the national security policy apparatus through his direct line authority over the premier (whom he appoints without confirmation of the legislative branch and who possesses formal line authority over the operations of government national security organs such as the Ministry of Foreign Affairs and the Ministry of National Defense[1]), and through his direct administrative supervision over two critical national security organs within the Office of the President: the NSC and its subordinate NSB.[2] The president also exercises authority over the national security (and defense) policy apparatus through a direct connection to the supreme operational organ of the ROC military: the GSH.[3]

The latter feature of this structure of presidential control in the national security/defense arena (i.e., the direct president-GSH relationship) derives from the formal direct link that exists between the president and the chief of the general staff (CGS) under Taiwan's existing national defense decisionmaking structure. On the basis of the 1970 Ministry of National Defense Organization Law (*guofangbu zuzhifa*) and the 1978 Ministry of National Defense General Staff Organization Law (*guofangbu canmoubenbu zuzhifa*), Taiwan's defense

---

[1]The president's influence over these bodies is further reinforced by the fact that he appoints all state ministers, on the recommendation of the premier.

[2]Two other organs within the Office of the President with potential influence over national security policy issues are the National Unification Council (NUC) and the National Unification Research Council (NURC). Founded in 1990, the NUC consists of 30+ leaders in various fields, from both government and private sectors, organized into task groups. According to *The Republic of China Yearbook, 1997* (p. 77), the NUC recommends national unification policies to the president, helps the government to devise a national unification framework, and builds consensus within society and among Taiwan's political parties concerning the issue of national unification. In reality, however, the NUC has little real policy influence. It rarely meets and functions primarily to support the president's position on national unification issues. Most notably, it reportedly plays no significant role in shaping the president's views on national security strategy or defense issues. The NURC is an ad hoc organization established by President Lee Teng-hui as an informal advisory body on Mainland issues. It provides some genuine, *albeit secondary*, policy input in areas relating to national security strategy.

[3]The specific features of presidential policy interactions with these national security organs are discussed below.

decisionmaking apparatus was divided into two systems:   the military command system (*junling xitong*) and the military administration system (*junzheng xitong*).   In the latter system, defense policies are carried out through a chain of command comprising the president, the premier, the minister of national defense, and the chief of the general staff.   Under the former system, the president directly commands the armed forces through the chief of the general staff.   Under this authority system (and unlike most democratic presidential or parliamentary systems), the ROC president exercises direct military command authority (*junling*) over the CGS regarding "operational matters."[4]   Regarding more routine, administrative issues (*junzheng*), the CGS is directly subordinate to the minister of national defense.

The president exercises his authority over the CGS through both private interactions and a more formal policy channel, consisting of a regularly convened military discussion meeting (*junshi huitan*).   This direct link to the CGS permits the president to exercise direct command authority over the military without passing through the office of the minister of national defense.   It also, at least until very recently, prevented close scrutiny of the activities of the GSH by the Executive Yuan and, indirectly, the Legislative Yuan.[5]   However, a proposed reform of the ROC National Defense Organization Law currently under consideration by the Legislative Yuan is designed to place the

---

[4]The president-CGS link originally arose as a logical reflection of the extensive military leadership role performed by ROC President Chiang Kai-shek during the prolonged armed struggle with the communists on the Chinese Mainland.   This link will be discussed in greater detail in Chapter Three.

[5]Under the ROC Constitution, the Legislative Yuan (LY) can supervise the premier as the highest official in the executive branch but not the president.   Hence, the president's direct link to the CGS places the latter, as chief of staff to the president for operational matters, within the orbit of presidential authority and therefore arguably beyond the reach of legislative oversight.   Indeed, during the past 50 years, chiefs of the general staff have invariably declined invitations from the LY to report on military affairs.   In recent years, however, the refusal by the CGS to report to the LY has become more and more unacceptable to legislators and the general public.   As a result, the Council of Grand Justices (a supra-Supreme Court that exists to interpret the ROC Constitution and provide unified interpretations of laws and ordinances) affirmed in July 1998 that the CGS, as an official of the executive branch, cannot refuse to report to committee meetings of the LY.   However, the council also ruled that the CGS is not required to attend or answer queries at the plenary session of the LY, because he is not a member of the cabinet.   Following this ruling, General Tang Fei, when he served as CGS, appeared before the LY.   See Ding and Huang (1998).

CGS entirely under the Ministry of National Defense and ultimately the premier and hence remove an important channel of presidential control over the uniformed military (while also making the military directly subject to LY supervision).[6]

The current president of the ROC is Lee Teng-hui. Initially promoted to the presidency in 1988 upon the death of Chiang Ching-kuo, Lee is the first popularly elected head of state in Chinese history (that election was held in March 1996). Although responsible for the broad contours of Taiwan's national security strategy, foreign policy, and defense policy, President Lee's attention and expertise in the national security realm are by all accounts primarily focused on non-military issues, especially (a) the major features of Taiwan's multi-pronged effort to increase its international profile (and hence its level of international support) via his strategy of pragmatic (or flexible) diplomacy, and (b) the general contours of Taiwan's increasing diplomatic, economic, and political interactions with the PRC. Moreover, Lee's approach to these two interrelated pillars of Taiwan's foreign policy are greatly influenced by his domestic political calculations and objectives, especially his perception of what is required to maintain power and ensure his historical legacy in an environment marked by the increasing influence over the political process of native Taiwanese and the associated growth of pro-independence sentiments on Taiwan.

Lee's approach to military and defense issues derives primarily from the security implications or requirements of these external and internal sets of priorities. From Lee's viewpoint, pragmatic diplomacy and the island's growing cross-strait relationship with an increasingly strong China require both the maintenance of an effective military deterrence and, if possible, closer security relations with the United States and Japan.[7] Both goals are essential, in Lee's view, not only to maintain the security of Taiwan but also to strengthen his general level of support among the non-Mainlander Taiwanese

---

[6]This important point is discussed in greater detail in Chapter Three.

[7]Lee is reportedly very supportive of efforts to establish concrete defense cooperation with the United States and Japan, such as direct defense dialogues and consultations and coordination and communication between each country's air and naval forces. Some observers also insist that Lee favors Taiwan participation in a U.S.- and Japan-led multilateral security structure for the region.

populace.  Whether Lee's ultimate objective in supporting a strong Taiwan with closer security ties to the West is to create the conditions for formal Taiwan independence from the Mainland is a matter of debate among observers.  Many believe that, at the very least, Lee is pushing to establish some level of international acceptance of Taiwan as an equal, separate, and sovereign entity, both to consolidate his party's domestic political base and his personal historical legacy and to provide Taiwan with greater leverage in a future negotiation for the establishment of a loose confederation-type relationship with Beijing (e.g., a voluntary "Union of Chinese States" similar to the Commonwealth of Independent States (CIS) of the former Soviet Union).

Within the Office of the President, an array of special advisors and deputy advisors to the president provide expert advice on a wide variety of subjects.  However, the actual policy influence of these individuals depends greatly upon their individual stature and connections within the government and, most important, on their personal relationship with the president.  At present, of 16 senior advisors, only Ding Mau-shih reportedly exercises significant influence over national security-related policy issues.  A Mainlander (from Yunan Province) with extensive foreign ministry experience and a former secretary-general of the NSC, Ding is widely regarded as a highly capable and personable individual with close personal ties to the president.[8]  As a result of his influence and status, Ding was asked by Lee Teng-hui to remain in the administration as a senior presidential advisor after retiring from the NSC in early 1999.  His high status within the Lee Teng-hui administration is indicated by the fact that he is currently the only senior presidential advisor to have an office within the presidential office building (*zongtongfu*).[9]

As a senior presidential advisor, Ding takes major responsibility for overseeing relations with the United States and other major foreign

---

[8]One interviewee stated that some consider Ding to be the senior representative of a so called informal "Mainlander Group" within Lee Teng-hui's government.

[9]Ding's office was previously occupied by Jiang Yan-shih, a former secretary-general of the Office of the President.

policy issues.[10]  He accompanies all foreign guests when they meet with Lee Teng-hui.  Although arguably exercising as much (or perhaps more) influence over policy toward the United States as either Foreign Minister Jason Hu or NSC Secretary-General Yin Tsung-wen, it is unclear how and to what extent Ding influences Lee's foreign policy views.  What is clear, however, is that Ding does not exert much influence over purely defense-related national security issues.

The vice president of the Republic of China does not exercise much power within the ROC political system.  Most notably, he does not have any formal, direct authority over key national security organs.  Hence, his influence within the national security policy arena is largely informal or ex officio, deriving primarily from his potential role as a key personal advisor to the president.  The significance of his role largely depends on his overall personal stature and his relationship to the president.  The current vice president, Lien Chan, is regarded as a close personal associate to Lee Teng-hui and is his designated successor as president.  However, Lien Chan by all accounts has little knowledge of or interest in defense-related national security matters.  His advice to President Lee and his expertise focus primarily on domestic politics and, to a lesser extent, foreign affairs.

## Office of the Premier of the Executive Yuan

The premier of the ROC is appointed by the president (without confirmation by the Legislative Yuan) and is thus highly dependent upon the latter's support and good will.[11]  However, the premier exercises a significant level of formal and informal authority over national policy, including national security policy.  The latter derives, as in the case of the vice president, primarily from his potential role as a key advisor to the president.  The former, more significant authority derives from the premier's position as the highest official of the executive branch:  The premier is president of the Executive Yuan, the

---

[10]Ding is supported in these efforts by Dr. Lin Bih-jaw, one of two deputy secretaries-general within the Office of the President. Lin was a former deputy director of the NSC and was also transferred to the Office of the President in early 1999.

[11]Indeed, knowledgeable observers of Taiwan's national defense apparatus have referred to the premier as the president's protégé and proxy in carrying out policy.

supreme executive body in charge of administering all the major organs of government.  In the national security arena, the premier's formal power exists largely as a function of (1) his line authority over the Ministry of Foreign Affairs, the Ministry of Defense, and the Mainland Affairs Council (the latter established in 1990 to handle the growing contacts with the Chinese Mainland), (2) his direction, under the ultimate authority of the president, of a national government policy deliberation and formulation process centered on the Executive Yuan, and (3) his position as one of two vice chairmen of the National Security Council within the Office of the President (the ROC vice president is the other vice chairman).

Although the premier arguably exerts significant levels of influence within all three areas, his input is by all accounts not absolutely decisive to the formulation of core national security policies in any area.  Moreover, his authority over line ministries is limited largely to supervisory duties and does not entail substantive policymaking functions, although the premier can certainly influence the specifics of ministerial policy at times.  Overall, the concrete, operational strategies and concepts guiding Taiwan's national security and foreign and defense policies are developed primarily by the respective ministries and through a wider variety of higher-level interactions between the president and the other senior civilian and military leaders discussed in this chapter.

The premier-led Executive Yuan policy process is largely ad hoc and designed to bring a variety of senior officials and experts together to deliberate over a particular policy issue and to generate policy analyses and recommendations for the president.  This process can at times include military figures and involve defense-related concerns.  However, it is normally most concerned with domestic or particular foreign policy issues and hence does not play a decisive role in the larger national security (or defense) policy process.[12]  The premier

---

[12]The main policy agencies employed in this arena are ad hoc special task forces of officials and experts organized by the premier's office to examine a specific policy issue and produce required support for the president.  Such a task force, including both military and nonmilitary members, was reportedly formed during the period of increased political and military tension with Beijing during summer 1995–spring 1996. A special task force on cross-strait relations also reportedly exists and is coordinated by the Mainland Affairs Council (MAC).  All such task forces report directly to the premier.

serves primarily as the organizer, supervisor, and facilitator of this Executive Yuan process, on behalf of the president.[13]

The premier's membership on the NSC is of no great consequence to national security and defense matters largely because the NSC *as a body* is not a critical player in these arenas, although its influence could grow in the future, as discussed below.

On balance, as with many other senior national leaders, the premier's importance to the national security policy process is largely a function of his overall political clout in the ROC government and his personal relationship with the president. The present premier of the ROC is Vincent Siew. According to most interviewees, Premier Siew's influence over national security strategy is extremely limited. Although considered by many as enjoying a reasonably close personal relationship with Lee Teng-hui, Siew reportedly does not provide critical national security or defense policy advice to the president. Instead, as with Vice President Lien Chan, his advice focuses more on issues relating to domestic politics and to a lesser extent on foreign affairs. His role in the national security or defense arena is thus largely as a general supervisor of the three above-outlined areas of responsibility.

## National Security Council

Originally established in 1967 and subsequently restructured through an amendment of the ROC Constitution in April 1991, the NSC (*guojia anquan huiyi*) is an advisory body to the president formally charged with determining the ROC's national security policies

---

[13]Two other Executive Yuan bodies also merit note: the Executive Yuan Council and the Executive Plan plenary meetings. The former is a policymaking organization comprising the premier (who presides over its meetings), the vice premier, ministers of state, the heads of the ROC's eight ministries, and the heads of the Mongolian and Tibetan Affairs Commission and the Overseas Chinese Affairs Commission. The council discusses and decides on statutory and budgetary bills and bills concerning martial law, amnesty, declarations of war, conclusion of peace or other treaties and other issues, which are to be submitted to the Legislative Yuan, as well as matters of common concern to the various ministries and commissions. Hence, it does not play a significant role in national security policy deliberations or formulation. The latter is convened weekly and is attended by more than 50 individuals, including Democratic Progressive Party (DPP) politicians. Such a large and diverse forum does not perform a meaningful role in the national security policy process.

and assisting in planning the ROC's security strategy.[14]  Within this broad mandate, the NSC plays a policy role within a wide variety of areas, including foreign affairs, relations with the Mainland, military defense, foreign intelligence collection and analysis, and domestic security and counterintelligence.[15]  Of these functions, the most important for external national security policy are (1) cross-strait relations, (2) foreign policy, and (3) national defense policy.  Although small (with an internal staff of fewer than 60), the NSC exercises formal supervisory authority over much larger national-security-related organizations.  The most important of these for external national security affairs is the NSB, discussed below.

The NSC consists of a senior membership and is supported by a Secretariat.  The senior NSC membership includes the president, as NSC chairman, and the vice president and premier, who serve as NSC vice chairmen.  Other senior members of the NSC include the ministers of foreign affairs, national defense, and economic affairs, the NSC secretary-general, the director of the Mainland Affairs Council, the director of the National Security Bureau, and the general-secretary of the Office of the President.  The NSC Secretariat serves as a "staff office to coordinate inter-agency implementation of NSC policy directives, channel intelligence from the intelligence community to the NSC and prepare the agenda for NSC meetings."[16]  It is headed by a secretary-general and three deputy secretaries-general.  The three deputies are each responsible for one of the three main national security policy areas mentioned above.  The NSC Secretariat also contains from five to seven NSC advisors or chancellors, several of whom conduct research and produce policy recommendations concerning the above three functional areas.

Seemingly impressive on paper, the NSC as a body is not at present a major actor in the national security policy process and in particular has very little influence over defense-related matters.  Under the NSC Organization Law promulgated after the 1991 constitutional

---

[14]*The Republic of China Yearbook 1997*, p. 77.  The formal authority of the NSC was reconstituted in 1991 when its legal basis was cast into doubt following the lifting of martial law and the termination of the Temporary Provisions During the Period of Mobilization Against Communist Rebellion.

[15]Shambaugh (1996), p. 1289.

[16]Shambaugh (1996), p. 1289.

amendments, the NSC was designated merely as a consultative agency for the president with no decisionmaking or interagency co-ordination powers.  Given its relatively weak authority, the senior membership of the NSC rarely meet as a body.[17]  Whereas the U.S. NSC normally coordinates national security policy across the many relevant agencies of the executive branch, in the ROC, most national security policy coordination occurs elsewhere, if at all.  Although the NSC deputy secretaries-general meet fairly regularly with subordinate researchers and advisors to discuss their specific areas of policy responsibility, many members of the NSC Secretariat are retired military or civilian officials with little policy influence, and the number of NSC researchers and advisors is limited by law to a mere handful. Moreover, each researcher functions with little or no support staff. The extreme weakness of the NSC in the defense policy arena is suggested by the fact that the NSC does not filter military intelligence or provide defense policy recommendations for the senior civilian leadership, despite the NSC's formal supervisory authority over the NSB. Those few NSC staff members with defense policy responsibilities (e.g., the NSC deputy secretary-general in charge of defense matters), reportedly are not very active.

Hence, overall, the NSC is significant primarily as a source of individual advice and expertise to the ROC president.  In this regard, by far the most influential figure within the NSC is the secretary-general. As the most senior national security official within the Office of the President, the NSC secretary-general functions as the president's primary national security advisor.  However, as with other senior positions, the extent of his influence on national security and defense policy issues depends very much on the type and level of his policy expertise and his personal relationship with the president.

The current NSC secretary-general is retired General Yin Tsung-wen, the former head of the NSB and an individual with extensive experience in both the military and intelligence arenas.  Yin assumed office in early 1999, replacing the highly competent and trusted Ding Mau-shih.  Some observers believe that Yin Tsung-wen was selected by Lee Teng-hui to replace Ding to greatly strengthen the influence of

---

[17]Under the law, the president can convene select subgroups of the senior NSC membership.  However, Lee Teng-hui reportedly rarely calls such meetings.

the NSC within the defense policy arena.  Others vigorously reject such an assessment, citing the above-mentioned institutional constraints to such a development, Lee's presumed desire to maintain sole civilian oversight regarding military matters, and the continued dominance of the military over basic decisions taken within this arena.[18]  At the very least, it is clear that Yin Tsung-wen is attempting, with Lee Teng-hui's strong support, to integrate the activities of the NSC more closely with those of the NSB by enhancing the quality and amount of intelligence provided to the former by the latter.[19]

## Ministry of Foreign Affairs

The MoFA is the supreme national government organ responsible for the foreign relations of the ROC.  Its activities are primarily limited to the formulation and implementation of civilian policies associated with diplomatic and political relations with foreign states and international organizations.  The MoFA's leading official, the foreign minister, has some influence over the setting of national security strategy and defense-related policies through various formal and informal interactions with the president and the premier, including private consultations with the president, his involvement in the Executive-Yuan-centered policy process and in the policy deliberations of the Kuomintang Central Committee (discussed below), and through his membership on the NSC.  In general, however, the foreign minister is not a pivotal actor in the formulation of Taiwan's broader national security strategy and has virtually no influence over defense policies.  Current Foreign Minister Jason Hu is a very capable, cosmopolitan official with extensive experience in foreign affairs and especially in handling relations with the United States.

---

[18]It is commonly known that Yin Tsung-wen wanted the minister of national defense slot, replacing Chiang Chung-ling.  However, Lee eventually rejected this option because many senior military officers believed that Yin had been away from the military arena for too long.  Moreover, it would have been unprecedented for a NSB head to become minister of defense.

[19]In addition, General Yin is reportedly proceeding to augment the staff size of the NSC and has proposed to the LY that it modify the existing law to permit the NSC to develop a full-fledged analytical unit.  There are also reports that support is growing within the LY to strengthen the overall authority and influence of the NSC within the national security policy process.

He reportedly has no significant experience or influence in the defense policy arena, however.

## Ministry of National Defense

The MND is the supreme government agency responsible for national defense. Its primary duties and functions (enumerated in Chapter Three) thus center on the narrower realm of defense policy and military maintenance and development. In fact, the primary institutional role of the MND is limited to exercising administrative oversight of the military and to facilitating and coordinating military interactions with the civilian side of government on critical matters such as the defense budget. Hence, the MND as an institution does not exercise much creative power over broader aspects of national security policy.

The major components of national security policy are determined by the president in consultation with other senior civilian and military leaders. Thus, ultimately, the power and influence of the MND over national security strategy depends greatly on the authority of the minister of national defense. Taiwan's defense minister exerts significant potential influence over the setting of both national security strategy and defense policy through his interactions with the president (as commander-in-chief and head of state) and the premier (as head of the executive branch). These include private consultations with the president, his direct involvement in the Executive-Yuan-centered policy process and in the policy deliberations of the Kuomintang Central Committee, and, to a lesser degree, through his membership on the NSC.

Former CGS General Tang Fei succeeded retired General Chiang Chung-ling as minister of national defense in February 1999. General Tang is a highly capable and well-respected Air Force general with a keen strategic mind.[20]  From February 1998 to January 1999, he served as chief of the general staff (replacing General Lo Ben-li, an

---

[20]Tang reportedly played a major role in a provisional policymaking committee formed during the 1995–96 military confrontation with the PLA and is an astute advocate of greater operational jointness and improvements in Taiwan's air defense system.

Army general)[21] and before that was executive vice chief of the general staff. The rapid promotion of Tang Fei, a Mainlander, from executive vice CGS to CGS and then to minister of national defense was a surprise to most observers, who expected Lee Teng-hui to favor either a native Taiwanese or a close personal confidante for the posts of CGS and defense minister.[22] Lee probably promoted Tang to these positions because of the latter's high competence, especially in the areas of defense strategy, military modernization,[23] and military restructuring, and because of his apparent sensitivity to both the larger political environment on Taiwan and to the complex Taiwan-U.S.-PRC relationship. Tang has excellent relations with the U.S. military, for example. In addition, the Mainlander-dominated senior officer corps of the ROC Army has long been regarded by many observers as a bulwark of conservatism and an opponent to Lee's broader aims of opening up the military to greater public scrutiny and of promoting more native Taiwanese officers to high rank. Tang Fei will probably serve as a strong ally in these efforts. Some interviewees also suggest that Tang's promotion to defense minister occurred in part as a result of his support for Taiwan's participation in a U.S.-led TMD system, a move apparently strongly favored by Lee Teng-hui and opposed by some segments of the military.

## General Staff Headquarters

Overall, the GSH as an institution exerts enormous influence over the formulation and implementation of Taiwan's military strategy and defense doctrine, force structure, and budget/procurement policies, as discussed in greater detail in Chapter Three. As with the MND, in the broader arena of national security strategy, the influence of the

---

[21]The CGS post normally rotates every two years among the three armed services. General Lo held the position for nearly three years, however.

[22]Many expected that Lee Teng-hui would select General Huang Hsien-jung, former ROC Air Force commander-in-chief and a native Taiwanese, as CGS, and Admiral Chuang Ming-yao, the current ROC representative to Japan, a former commander-in-chief (CinC) of the ROC Navy, and a close associate of President Lee, as minister of national defense.

[23]Tang is considered by some observers to be a major driving force behind the efforts of the ROC military to improve its capabilities in critical software areas such as doctrine, training, jointness, and C3I, and in air defense. These efforts are discussed in greater detail below.

GSH is primarily exerted through its head, the CGS. As the senior ROC official responsible for military doctrine and readiness, and with a direct channel to the president regarding operational military matters, the CGS has the potential to exert significant influence over defense-related national security issues and policies. However, the CGS does not normally participate in those broader national policy fora open to more senior leaders (i.e., the Executive-Yuan-centered policy process, the Kuomintang Central Committee process, and the deliberations of the NSC), and his formal responsibilities are limited to the military defense arena. These factors suggest that the overall influence of the CGS on broader national security policy issues outside of the narrower realms of defense policy and strategy, force structure, military operations, and procurement issues would highly depend upon the specific nature of his relationship with the president and, to a lesser extent, with the minister of national defense.

The new CGS is former Army Commander-in-Chief General Tang Yao-ming, who replaced Tang Fei in February 1999. Although intelligent and highly motivated, many observers believe that Tang was chosen as CGS primarily because he is one of the ROC's few senior military officers of Taiwanese origin. Lee Teng-hui has reportedly wanted to fill the CGS post with a non-Mainlander for quite some time and shifted Tang Fei to the MND post in part to achieve this goal. Before his promotion as Army commander-in-chief, Tang Yao-ming's career was largely in the political work arena. No interviewees indicated that General Tang plays a significant role in the formulation of basic national security policy.

## National Security Bureau

The NSB is the supreme national government organ responsible for collecting and processing both civilian and military intelligence. Under the law, the NSB primarily oversees intelligence relevant to external national security issues, including intelligence collection and analysis toward the PRC.[24] The NSB reportedly employs approx-

---

[24]The National Security Act of 1993 placed the previous domestic security and counterintelligence functions of the NSB primarily within the Investigation Bureau of

imately 1,500 personnel and comprises six internal departments (Mainland Operations, Overseas Operations, Internal Security Intelligence, Research and Production, Communications, and Cypher). It also has operational sections for scientific research (including signals intelligence) and data processing.[25] Beyond these internal functions and responsibilities, the NSB also guides, coordinates, and supports the intelligence affairs of the Military Intelligence Bureau of the Ministry of National Defense, the Telecommunications Development Division, the Coastal Defense Headquarters, the Military Police Headquarters, the National Police Administration of the Interior Ministry, and the Investigation Bureau of the Justice Ministry.

Given its primary function as an intelligence organ, the NSB as an institution exerts little direct influence over the formulation or implementation of national security or defense policies. However, the director of the NSB has the potential to significantly influence such policy arenas, as a result of his direct involvement in senior policy organs, his military background, and his relationship with the president. The NSB director is normally a three-star general, equivalent in rank to a vice chief of staff and a service commander-in-chief. He is also a member of the NSC. Most significantly, however, the NSB director also reports directly to the president, despite the fact that the NSB is administratively supervised by the NSC. This link is important primarily as a source of policy-related intelligence but can also sometimes have broader relevance for policymaking, depending on the personal relationship between the president and the NSB director. Overall, however, the director of the NSB almost certainly wields less defense-related policy influence at senior levels of the government than does either the minister of national defense or the chief of the general staff.

The current NSB director is General Ding Yu-zhou, a Mainlander from Shandong. Widely regarded as a very capable officer, Ding is a former field commander and head of the Military Intelligence Bureau (J-2). The new director's relation to others in the national security apparatus is not yet clear.

---

the Ministry of Justice and placed the NSB under the administrative direction of the NSC. See Shambaugh (1996), p. 1290.

[25]Shambaugh (1996), p. 1290.

In addition to the above seven core national security institutions and leaders, two other sets of institutions merit some mention as important, albeit clearly secondary, actors within the national security policy apparatus. These organs are associated with Taiwan's political parties and representative political institutions.

## The Kuomintang Standing Committee and Advisory Committees

The Nationalist Party (Kuomintang) Central Committee is represented by a Central Standing Committee when the former is not in session. The Standing Committee contains most senior national government officials (who are also senior KMT members), including the president, the premier, the minister of foreign affairs, the NSC secretary-general, and the minister of national defense, among others. The committee meets weekly to deliberate and approve important policies for the party and the government and to nominate individuals for important party and government positions, including ministers and vice ministers.[26] This forum thus serves to bring together senior national security officials, including the president, on a frequent basis, and has the potential to play a significant role in the national security policy process. Most observers insist, however, that meetings of the KMT Standing Committee discuss domestic issues almost exclusively; on those rare occasions when external policy is considered, the focus of the discussion is foreign policy, not defense policy. Overall, no interviewees pointed to the KMT Standing Committee as an important actor in the national security policy process.

The KMT Central Committee also develops national security policy proposals for the Office of the President through the less formal mechanism of an advisory committee. Such KMT committees exist for a wide range of policy subjects, including, in the national security arena, foreign policy, defense policy, and cross-strait relations (thus mirroring the major functional divisions within the NSC, noted above). Each committee is composed of very senior KMT politicians, retired KMT government officials, and some key serving agency heads, such as the director of the MAC, and functions under the

---

[26]*The Republic of China Yearbook 1997*, p. 100.

oversight of the secretary-general of the KMT. The primary purpose of such committees is to generate policy analysis and present policy recommendations to the president, in his capacity as chairman of the KMT.

During the Lee Teng-hui administration, these KMT-based avenues of policy deliberation and advice have reportedly played a decreasingly important role in policymaking, for two reasons. First, the KMT's overall level of influence within the ROC government has declined significantly in recent years as other political parties, such as the generally pro-independence DPP, have garnered increasing levels of public support as a consequence of the overall democratization process. As a result of such changes, other political parties have increased their influence on government policies whereas purely KMT policy structures have encountered increasing criticism from opposition political parties and much of the public. Second, Lee Teng-hui has reportedly become less inclined to use KMT policy channels because of the growth of internal policy schisms within the KMT and because he is less trusting of the KMT apparatus in general, a significant segment of which opposes his efforts to Taiwanize the political process and to push forward with his foreign policy strategy of pragmatic diplomacy.

### The Foreign and Overseas Affairs and National Defense Committees of the Legislative Yuan

In the past, the LY exerted little independent influence over national security matters. Those legislative committees responsible for policies in these areas, most notably the National Defense Committee and the Foreign and Overseas Affairs Committee, were completely under the control of the KMT and supported the needs and interests of the KMT-led military and the KMT-led civilian government. For example, the LY National Defense Committee was controlled by a small clique of pro-military KMT members, who resisted revealing any information about national security or defense matters to the entire LY. According to some interviewees, such conservative KMT control allegedly contributed greatly to excessive secrecy and corruption in the military sector, illustrated by the series of procurement scandals that emerged in the mid 1990s.

However, in the mid 1990s, the Legislative Yuan became a more important, independent actor in the national security arena, largely as a consequence of the increasing strength of non-KMT political parties within the government and the concomitant emergence of popular sentiment critical of the tight hold the KMT has exerted over defense matters in the past.  Moreover, serious procurement scandals in the military, with sensational side effects, gained notoriety during that period and forced greater legislative attention to reform measures and efforts to ensure that reforms enacted were implemented.[27]  As a result of these developments, stronger attempts have been made to gain greater civilian control and legislative oversight over the military and defense matters in general.  This process has been notably marked not by greater LY involvement in areas relating to broader national security strategy but, at least until recently,[28] by increasing levels of LY scrutiny of the defense budget and procurement process, and by more frequent interpolations before the LY National Defense and Foreign and Overseas Affairs Committees.[29]

## THE NATIONAL SECURITY POLICY PROCESS

As suggested by the above presentation of Taiwan's major national security policy actors, no formal, institutionalized, and regularized interagency process or mechanism for national security strategy formulation and implementation exists that spans all the key senior civilian and military agencies and policymakers.[30]  In other words, the ROC government has no equivalent to the U.S. National Security Council or the Principals Meetings that bring together key U.S. agency heads to discuss and determine specific national security policy on a regular basis.  Moreover, at lower levels of the policy pro-

---

[27]Shambaugh (1996), p. 1296.

[28]The level of LY influence over defense matters reportedly began to decline somewhat in the late 1990s.  This development is discussed in Chapter Three.

[29]Shambaugh (1996), pp. 1293, 1296.

[30]Moreover, no single agency coordinates the production and dissemination of civilian and military national security policy research and analysis.  Primary producers of such products include the National Security Council, the National Security Bureau, the Mainland Affairs Council, the Ministry of Foreign Affairs, the Ministry of Economic Affairs, and various outside research institutes with close government connections, such as the Institute for National Policy Research (INPR).

cess, no formal institutions exist to provide ongoing policy coordination and implementation of national-level grand strategies among civilian and defense policy sectors. Most notably, there is no formal, institutionalized structure of policy interaction between MoFA and MND leaders and offices. Many people in uniform consider it unnecessary to inform MoFA officials about national defense and security (*guofang anquan*) issues and many MoFA officials regard military officers as uninformed and insufficiently sensitive to political and international relations issues.

This lack of regularized policy interaction between senior civilian and military officials and organizations means that national security strategy is developed either on a fragmentary basis, within individual responsible agencies, or by the president alone, through largely separate, and often private, interactions with senior civilian and military officials and advisors. On balance, policy coordination and integration on broad national security matters (including national strategic objectives and the major principles guiding both foreign and defense policies) are extremely weak and depend almost entirely on the initiative and determination of the president.

In general, the president can employ two major types of channels or fora to receive analysis and advice, convey directives and instructions, and facilitate policy consultations, deliberations, and coordination in the national security policy arena: ad hoc, informal meetings with senior officials and advisors and limited bureaucratic policy mechanisms.

## Ad Hoc, Private Meetings

The first policy mechanism consists primarily of informal, private meetings with the six key national security figures discussed above. The ROC president has the authority to call such ad hoc meetings with any of these leaders at any time, either individually or in small groups. From a formal, institutional point of view, the most important such leadership interactions for overall national security policymaking are those with the premier, the minister of foreign affairs, and the minister of national defense. However, in reality, the relative importance of any leadership figure as a private interlocutor with the president regarding national security policy issues depends very much on his personal relationship with the latter. Lee Teng-hui reportedly communicates privately to varying degrees with all six national security leaders, as suggested above.[31] He consults with the minister of national defense, the minister of foreign affairs, and the chief of the general staff, either individually or together, at least once per week and often more frequently.[32]

In the area of national security policy relating to defense issues, the most critical senior leadership connections are between President Lee and both the MND and the CGS. During Chiang Chung-ling's tenure as defense minister, the Lee Teng-hui-MND link was reportedly the more important, given the close personal relationship between Lee and Chiang. Most of Lee's knowledge of and assessments of defense-related national security issues reportedly derived in large part from information and opinions provided by Chiang. Tang Fei's February 1999 promotion to the post of defense minister suggests that the Lee-MND link will probably remain critical, because of Tang Fei's competence and prestige within the armed forces, his commitment to carrying out major structural reforms, and the fact that the new CGS General Tang Yao-ming is reportedly not as influential a figure within the military as is Tang Fei.

It is likely that Lee's interactions with General Tang Yao-ming occur most frequently in the less personal and less private context of the military discussion meeting (*junshi huitan*). However, as discussed in Chapter Three, this meeting reportedly deals exclusively with narrower defense issues and does not play a significant role in larger national security policy deliberations.

Both NSC Secretary-General General Yin Tsung-wen and Foreign Minister Jason Hu reportedly interact frequently with President Lee, especially regarding foreign affairs and cross-strait relations. NSB Director Ding Yu-zhou reports to President Lee both directly and indirectly via Yin Tsung-wen (given the fact that the NSC now exercises general oversight of the NSB). This personal link is important primarily as a source of policy-related intelligence, however. General

---

[31]To the author's knowledge, Lee Teng-hui does not consult privately, and regularly, on national security matters with senior government officials other than the six discussed in this chapter.

[32]President Lee also reportedly receives a daily national security briefing.

Ding reportedly does not interact privately with President Lee on broader national security (or defense) policy matters.

President Lee presumably interacts privately with Premier Vincent Siew regarding national security policy matters on a fairly regular basis, largely because of the institutional significance of the premiership within the overall national security apparatus. The premier's authority in this area derives primarily from his line authority over the Ministry of Foreign Affairs, the Ministry of Defense, and the Mainland Affairs Council, his direction of the Executive Yuan policy deliberation and formulation process, and his position as one of two vice chairmen of the National Security Council. In addition, the premier is also a member of the above-mentioned military meeting convened by the president and chaired by the CGS. However, most interviewees stress that Vincent Siew's contacts with President Lee regarding national security policy are limited largely to his role as overseer of national-security-related task forces under the Executive Yuan, and to his involvement with the president in MND budget and procurement oversight. Premier Siew reportedly does not take a regular, active role in deliberations with President Lee regarding national security or defense strategy.

Beyond holding confidential meetings with the above six senior figures, President Lee also consults privately with a fairly wide range of scholars, businessmen, and personal friends on various policy matters including, presumably, national security affairs.[33] However, by all accounts Lee Teng-hui has no close personal serving or retired military advisors with whom he consults privately on a regular basis, with the sole exception of former Defense Minister Chiang Chung-ling.

Chiang, who retired in January 1999 and became an unofficial advisor to Lee Teng-hui, is still viewed by some observers as a notable figure in the national security policy process largely because of his close personal ties to Lee and the continued influence he enjoys within a large part of the uniformed military. Chiang is a retired four-star Army general. His close personal relationship with Lee originated from the Chiang Ch'ing-kuo (CCK) period, when both

---

[33]These include members of the Academia Sinica, Academia Historica, and the National Unification Council.

men were striving to enlarge their influence from very weak positions within the executive (Lee as a largely powerless second-in-command to CCK, and Chiang Chung-ling as CCK's chief military aide).  The relationship between the two men was reportedly cemented after Lee became president, when Chiang helped Lee in his protracted political struggle with retired General Hao Pocun, a former defense minister and KMT conservative.[34]  Although Lee now relies most heavily on Tang Fei for advice on defense policy and procurement issues, the general handling of the military, and relations with the Legislative Yuan concerning military issues, he reportedly continues to consult with Chiang.

An informal group of security policy advisors, known as the Strategy Advisory Committee (SAC) (*zhanlue guwen weiyuanhui*), supposedly provides national security advice to the president.  This body mostly comprises retired military officers.  However, according to several interviewees, the SAC does not wield any policy influence because it is primarily an honorific body composed of individuals whom President Lee wishes to treat with respect but place out of the policy mainstream, such as retired Mainlander generals unsympathetic to Lee's foreign policy objectives.  No other inner circle of national security advisors to the president exists at this time within the ROC government.  In addition, the military-held post of chief of staff (*canjun zhang*) within the Office of the President has been abolished, leaving only a chief aide-de-camp (*shiwei zhang*) as the sole senior military figure within the president's office.  However, this post reportedly possesses no policy role or influence whatsoever.

## Limited Bureaucratic Policy Mechanisms

As suggested above, three major policy coordination and consultation mechanisms exist in the national security bureaucracy to assist the president:  the NSC, the Executive Yuan policy deliberation and formulation process, and the KMT Central Committee policy channel.  None of these serves as a regular and decisive means of coordinating or formulating national security policy, however; rather, they usually serve, when requested to do so by the president, as a means

---

[34]Hao had resisted Lee's efforts to "Taiwanize" the KMT and also opposed his diplomatic line of so-called pragmatic or flexible diplomacy.

of generating policy advice and recommendations or of simply informing the president of the views of the bureaucracy. Moreover, at least one of these mechanisms, the NSC, rarely meets as a body, and both the Executive Yuan and KMT mechanisms usually address only domestic or narrow foreign policy issues (including cross-strait relations), not defense-related matters. The president, in consultation with the premier, chooses which of these three mechanisms to employ. Most recently, he has reportedly tended to rely more upon the Executive Yuan process.[35] However, no mechanism is employed on a regular basis as *the* formal policy channel or mechanism in national security affairs.

---

[35]According to one source, Lee Teng-hui has been very reluctant to increase the role of the NSC in national security affairs because of possible bureaucratic friction with the Executive Yuan. This might be changing, however. As indicated above, support is growing within the ROC government to increase the authority of the NSC as a policy formulation and coordination body within the overall national security policy process.

# Chapter Three

# DEFENSE POLICY, FORCE STRUCTURE, AND BUDGET/ PROCUREMENT DECISIONS

Although indirectly influenced by the above national security policy process, decisions to acquire specific foreign weapons platforms and related support systems are most consistently and directly influenced by the critical priorities, interests, and decisionmaking features of the ROC military's defense policymaking and procurement apparatus. Senior civilian and military leaders and organizations within this apparatus largely determine the major characteristics of Taiwan's defense strategy, operational doctrine, and desired force structure. These characteristics, in turn, combined with the influence exerted by broader political and policy considerations emanating from the larger national security policy arena, determine the specific budgetary and procurement decisions made regarding weapons platforms and related support systems.

## SENIOR ORGANIZATIONS AND LEADERS

The ROC defense policy, force structure, and budget/procurement decisionmaking apparatus is presented in Figure 2. This apparatus centers on five key institutions.

1. Office of the President
2. Ministry of National Defense

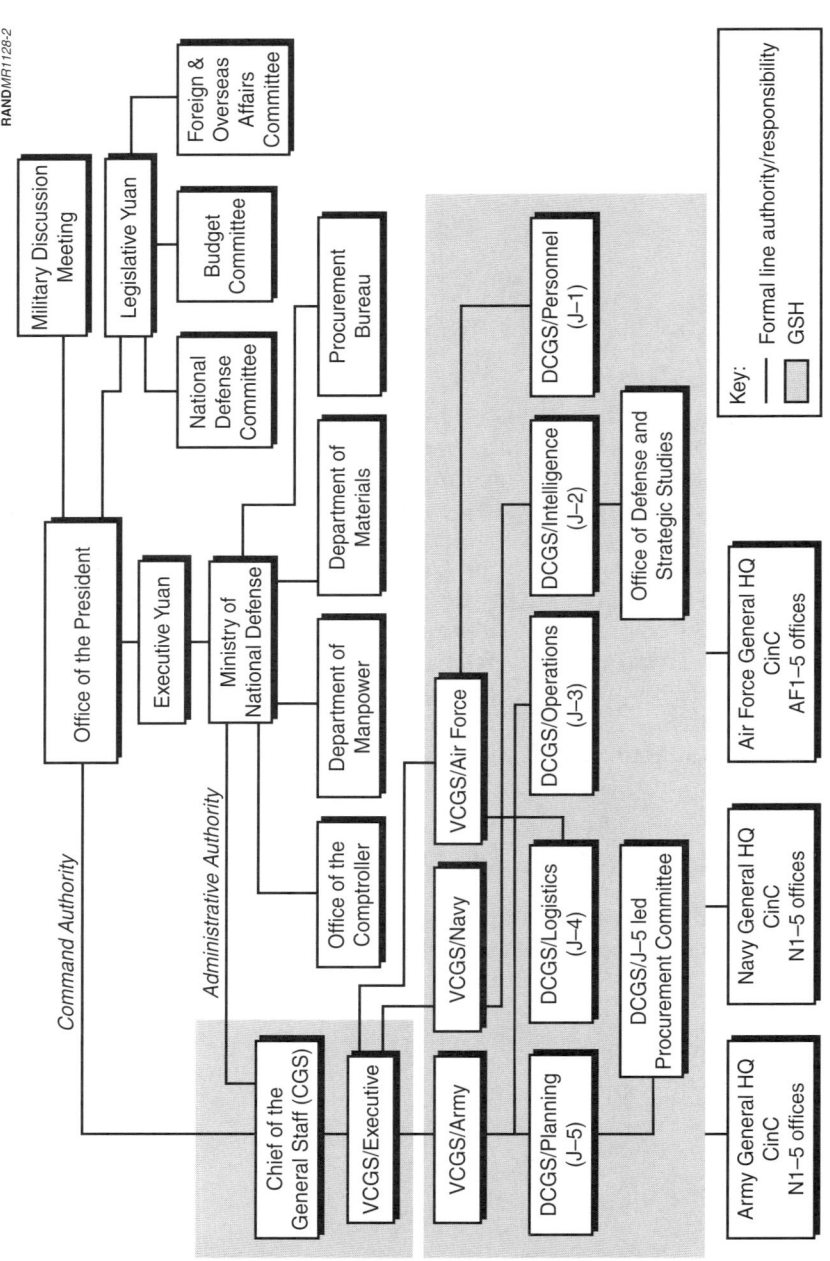

**Figure 2—Major Actors in the ROC Defense Policy Apparatus**

3. General Staff Headquarters

4. Armed Services General Headquarters

5. Legislative Yuan

## Office of the President

As part of his broad responsibilities as commander-in-chief of the armed forces and supreme authority regarding national security policy, the president of the Republic of China has the final word on defense policy and force structure issues and has the formal authority to oversee and intervene in budgetary and procurement decisions concerning major weapons systems. Theoretically, the ROC president is particularly well placed to play a decisive role in these areas because of the direct "command authority" link regarding operational matters that exists between himself and the CGS. Although the president's interactions with the CGS over operational matters is supposedly limited to control over specific military deployments and operations, in reality they can also include private deliberations over broader military issues such as Taiwan's defense strategy and force structure.

As noted in Chapter Two, Lee Teng-hui is clearly committed to the maintenance of an effective military. However, it is unclear whether Lee supports a strong military primarily for *political* purposes, as part of a larger strategy toward Beijing and Washington, or primarily for genuine *warfighting* purposes, to deter or defeat a possible attack from the Mainland. Each viewpoint suggests a very different presidential approach to force modernization and procurement.

The former perspective would largely derive from three key assumptions. First, Taiwan's security rests primarily upon the level of political and military support it receives from the United States and Japan. Second, any conflict with the Mainland would almost certainly require swift and forceful intervention by the United States if Taiwan were to survive, since Taiwan likely would not be able to mount an effective defense on its own for more than a few days or weeks at most. Third, Beijing recognizes that any use of force against Taiwan would pose dire consequences for regional stability and prosperity and hence seriously undermine its larger regional goals. As a result of these assumptions, Beijing is viewed as being highly unlikely to use direct military force against Taiwan, as long as the possibility of a strong and swift U.S. reaction exists—and would be at least very reticent to do so under almost any circumstances. Hence, at present, the military threat from Beijing is viewed as being largely political in nature, i.e., as part of a broader PRC strategy of coercive diplomacy designed to deter movement toward greater independence and to weaken U.S. political and military support for the island (in part by convincing the United States that the Taiwan issue is a matter of war or peace for Beijing). However, this type of threat (some would say bluff) does not presuppose an actual intention to attack Taiwan.

From this perspective, a strong ROC military is viewed primarily as a political instrument, i.e., to convey Taiwan's defiance, to reassure the Taiwan public that they are secure from Chinese military intimidation and coercion, and, most important, to strengthen U.S. ties with Taiwan. The last objective becomes increasingly important as China's capabilities increase and Taiwan's relative ability to provide for its own defense declines. Hence, Taiwan's armed forces are primarily seen as symbols of reassurance and resolve, not as key components of a larger force structure designed to attain genuine warfighting objectives; and U.S. weapons systems are valued primarily as critical indicators of greater U.S. support for the island. As a result of these assumptions, Taiwan should primarily emphasize the acquisition of highly visible and/or sophisticated weapons platforms, preferably from the United States, and place less emphasis on less-visible support systems and other forms of "software" essential to the creation of a serious warfighting capability.

The latter (warfighting) perspective would derive from an assumption that Beijing sees the utility of employing direct force against Taiwan and may indeed be preparing, not just threatening, to use such force in the future, and that the United States might not respond to a Chinese attack swiftly and forcefully enough to limit escalation and ensure Taiwan's security in the early stages of a conflict. Moreover, such a viewpoint probably also assumes that Beijing's willingness and ability to employ force will likely increase over time, thus potentially increasing the likelihood of a miscalculation leading to war. The logical conclusion drawn from this perspective is that Taiwan must create and maintain a military capable of repelling an attack from the Mainland and of holding on for an appreciable period of time, presumably until U.S. forces arrive. Hence, from this perspective, major foreign weapons platforms and their support systems should be evaluated on the basis of their true capability to successfully sustain ROC military resistance against a Mainland attack.

Many interviewees strongly suspect that President Lee adheres to the former viewpoint regarding the military threat from Beijing and how best to deal with it. They are particularly concerned that Lee underestimates the military danger posed by the PRC and overestimates the ability and willingness of the United States to come to Taiwan's assistance in the early stages of a conflict. It is extremely difficult to assess the validity of such suspicions. Taiwan's program of force modernization and its foreign procurement activities certainly seem to emphasize highly visible platforms. However, it seems unlikely that such decisions primarily reflect the influence of President Lee. With a few significant exceptions (discussed below), President Lee Teng-hui seems to leave most force structure and procurement decisions to the professional military. This, however, by no means ensures that such decisions will be made on the basis of a systematic, comprehensive, threat-driven assessment of Taiwan's warfighting needs, including both hardware and software.

Beyond his direct, personal link to the CGS, the president is also able to influence defense matters through his broader interactions with the ROC military leadership. These occur largely within the context of the military discussion meeting (*junshi huitan*). This meeting is convened by either the CGS or the president on an irregular basis and usually lasts approximately two hours. It is attended by the CGS (who normally chairs the meeting), the four vice chiefs of staff (including the executive vice chief of staff and the three vice chiefs), the defense minister, the premier, and the president. This forum reportedly provides a useful opportunity for the president to discuss the outlines of military affairs and defense policy and to pose questions to the military leadership.

In practice, however, Lee Teng-hui does not play a very active role in either oversight or decisionmaking regarding either the general features or specific contents of Taiwan's defense policy or force structure. He reportedly does not regularly and systematically supervise or intervene in shaping defense policy; nor does he seek to actively coordinate and integrate, either conceptually or operationally, the defense and foreign policy arenas.  Moreover, in general, Lee does not often intervene directly in budget or procurement decisions, especially given his limited time and technical knowledge of the issues involved.  In these matters, Lee usually receives information and guidance from Tang Fei, Chiang Chung-ling, and Tang Yao-ming.

In general, Lee's personal contacts with the CGS and the defense minister on defense matters reportedly consist primarily of either discussions regarding the handling of specific political issues relating to the military's relation to the LY or the resolution of very specific defense-related problems that require a presidential decision.  In addition, as with the NSC, the importance of the above-mentioned military discussion meeting to actual decisionmaking in the defense arena is significantly less than what appears on the surface.  The forum has no formal decisionmaking authority under the ROC Constitution.  Also, under Lee Teng-hui, the meeting usually does not deliberate over national security or defense policy or discuss in any detail Taiwan's force structure, defense budget, or military procurement process.  It normally consists of formal military briefings to the president (and the premier) on specific aspects of military readiness, organizational reform, or force development.  Potentially sensitive issues, including Taiwan's defense strategy or procurement process, are usually not covered in these briefings.  In other words, the meeting is normally convened to report military thinking and decisions to the president on relatively routine military matters, not to discuss sensitive issues or make decisions jointly with the president.[1]

Yet, as commander-in-chief of the armed forces, Lee Teng-hui possesses the authority to make major defense-related decisions and generally to influence the military decisionmaking process.  On occasion, he has been known to push particular issues, including procurement issues, largely because of their political or diplomatic importance, according to interviewees.  Perhaps the most notable example of such behavior is provided by Lee's increasingly strong

---

[1]The absence of an authoritative defense policymaking mechanism that brings together senior civilian and military officials will be at least partly remedied if a National Military Council (*guofang junshi huiyi*) is established through passage of the above mentioned National Defense Law.  This organ is discussed in greater detail below.

support for some type of sophisticated U.S.-supported theater missile defense system for Taiwan.[2]   Lee has long pressed for such a system despite the fact that significant elements of the ROC military are not enthusiastic about it, given its likely enormous cost, its unproven effectiveness, and its capacity to bring about a strong and highly unfavorable reaction from Beijing.  His motivation in doing so is presumably both to reassure the Taiwan public that there is (or could well be in the future) some means to defend against the growing ballistic missile threat to Taiwan posed by the Chinese and to strengthen defense ties with the United States.[3]   Until recently, military opposition to a TMD system, as well as public resistance,[4] had together served to check Lee's efforts.  However, both military and civilian support for some type of TMD system began to increase in late 1998/early 1999, especially after Tang Fei replaced Chiang Chung-ling as minister of national defense.  Chiang had reportedly held an extremely cautious attitude toward TMD, whereas Tang Fei has become a key supporter of such a system since assuming the post of defense minister.

---

[2]Such a system is designed to intercept exo-atmospheric ballistic missiles at high altitudes and would thus constitute a much more sophisticated and capable antimissile system than the existing so-called PAC 2+ variant of the Patriot system already supplied to Taiwan.  The latter is essentially a limited range "point" defense system primarily designed to intercept enemy aircraft, but with limited low-altitude antimissile capabilities.

[3]An effort to strengthen Taiwan's ties with the United States through the procurement of major U.S.-made weapons systems does not preclude support for the indigenous production of many weapons.  Indeed, according to some observers, Lee Teng-hui strongly favors the development of Taiwan's indigenous arms industry, in part to reduce Taipei's dependence on foreign suppliers for critical weapons such as missiles.

[4]Paradoxically, much of the Taiwan public reportedly opposes the placement of a TMD system in the vicinity of their homes and places of work, fearing that such deployments will attract Chinese ballistic missile attacks.  Apparently, the public understandably has little faith in the ability of such a system to provide sufficient protection against missile barrages.  This, at least in part, may explain the expressed preference by some senior Taiwan naval officials for a sea-based TMD system composed of at least four ships equipped with advanced Aegis air and missile defense systems (for detection, tracking, and target designation) plus interceptor missiles that remain under development by the U.S. Navy.

## Ministry of National Defense

The MND is the supreme government agency responsible for national defense. More specifically, it is formally responsible for "formulating military strategy, setting military personnel policies, devising draft and mobilization plans, delineating supply distribution policies, arranging for the research and development of military technology, compiling data for the national defense budget, setting military regulations, conducting court martial proceedings and administering military law."[5] The MND exercises administrative authority and direct civilian leadership[6] over the General Staff Headquarters, under which are the various armed services (see Figure 2).

In performing the above duties, the MND serves, on the one hand, as the major link between the uniformed military and the executive and legislative branches of the government and, on the other hand, as the primary administrative policy channel between the military and the president regarding defense matters. MND officials are thus normally responsible for explaining defense issues to civilian leaders and agencies (and to the general public) and also serve to coordinate, to some degree, defense policies and procedures with relevant nonmilitary policies and procedures. The MND performs a particularly important role in supervising, revising, and explaining the ROC defense budget and procurement process, through interactions with the Executive and Legislative Yuans and the uniformed military. The major MND offices responsible for budget and procurement functions are, respectively, the Office of the Comptroller and Departments of Manpower and Materials and the more recently established Procurement Bureau.

Despite its significant oversight and bureaucratic coordination responsibilities within the defense sector, the MND as an institution does not in fact play the lead role in formulating and revising defense policy or in determining Taiwan's force structure. The major elements of Taiwan's defense strategy/doctrine and related force structure are developed by the professional military, specifically the

---

[5] *The Republic of China Yearbook 1997*, p. 124.

[6] According to law, the minister of national defense must be a civilian, although a retired senior officer can, and currently does, hold this post.

GSH. The same is true regarding military budget and procurement decisions. Specifically, the MND seldom plays an active, independent role in shaping the size or content of the defense budget, largely because it does not have the internal expertise to scrutinize or challenge the details of budget requests submitted by the GSH. Hence, its primary responsibility is merely to oversee and review the preparation of the defense (and procurement) budgets by the professional military before they are submitted to the Executive Yuan for approval, and to respond to budget-related questions posed by the Legislative Yuan.

The MND Procurement Bureau was created in July 1995 by combining several military purchasing units, in response to public demands for greater transparency in and controls over the military's procurement process following the above-mentioned procurement scandals.[7] The bureau is formally responsible for "overall planning and purchasing [of] major weapons systems and equipment required by the ROC Armed Forces."[8] However, in reality, the MND Procurement Bureau reportedly plays only a minimal role in the procurement decisionmaking process. As in the general budgetary area, the bureau possesses no strong technical expertise regarding procurement matters. Most of the working level members of its sections and offices are administrative staffers from the GSH logistics (J-4) office. The primary task of the bureau is to oversee the implementation of contracts for acquisitions already determined through the internal GSH-directed procurement process discussed below, and to respond to questions regarding the procurement process posed by members of the Legislative Yuan.[9]

The overall limited role of the MND in the defense policy process derives in part from the historically dominant influence over the details of defense strategy, force structure, budget, and procurement decisions enjoyed by the armed services, especially the ROC Army. It

---

[7]Ibid., and *1996 National Defense Report, Republic of China* (1966), p. 96. The bureau contains five divisions, two sections, and one overseas foreign procurement unit.

[8]*The Republic of China Yearbook 1997*, p. 124.

[9]There are reports that General Tang Fei has moved to increase the influence of the MND Procurement Bureau over procurement policy since becoming minister of national defense. This has not been confirmed by the author, however.

also reflects the general historical importance of military leaders within the ROC political system. Moreover, the MND's capacity to play a leading role in determining core aspects of defense policy is constrained by the highly limited level of expertise residing within the offices of the MND. For example, the office of the minister of national defense includes no significant policy analysts or strategists and typically contains relatively few administrative personnel. Most defense-related policy and operational expertise remains firmly within the GSH and the individual armed services.[10]

The MND's formal authority over the military and its involvement in military planning and operational matters could increase, however, depending on the outcome of current efforts under way to revise the ROC National Defense Organization Law (renamed the National Defense Law in December 1997). These efforts include the proposal to eliminate the current direct link that exists, regarding operational matters, between the CGS and the president.[11] This revision would formally designate the minister of national defense as the senior government official in charge of *both* the military administration system and the military command system. Hence, under the proposed revision, the president would exercise his authority as commander-in-chief of the military indirectly, *via* the minister of national defense. This change would thus place the GSH and specifically the CGS *entirely* under the institutional authority of the MND and might thereby increase the ability of the MND to direct important aspects of de-

---

[10]One can speculate that this practice on Taiwan might be in part the perpetuation of habits inculcated before 1949; i.e., that the expertise for core military matters is resident in the general staff, not a ministry. I am indebted to Eric McVadon for this observation.

[11]The original draft revision of the National Defense Organization Law submitted by the MND to the Executive Yuan in September 1997 contained two versions. One maintained the current two-track "military command" and "military administration" systems. The second version recommended a convergence of the two systems. Given the sensitivity of this issue to questions of presidential authority and legislative oversight of the military, the EY sent both versions to the Office of the President for advice. Ultimately, Lee Teng-hui supported the convergence option. In a meeting of the KMT's Central Policy Commission on April 23, 1998, defense officials and KMT legislators, acting on a directive from KMT Chairman Lee Teng-hui, concluded that the MND should aim to achieve the convergence of the two military authority systems in drafting the new defense law. Accordingly, the MND submitted the convergence option to the EY on April 30, 1998, and the EY approved the option on May 21, 1998. The draft was submitted to the LY for review in the legislative session that began in September 1998. See Ding and Huang (1998) for details.

fense policy.[12]  In addition, further revisions of the draft National Defense Law undertaken since the original draft was submitted to the LY in September 1998[13] would reportedly place the service headquarters directly under the command of the MND and also greatly increase the number and functional expertise of MND agencies.  If enacted into law, these changes, combined with the convergence of military authority systems under the MND, would significantly shift control over basic military decisions from the GSH to the MND.[14]

## General Staff Headquarters

The GSH is the highest level agency in the ROC government responsible for military affairs.  It oversees the ROC Army, Navy, Air Force, Combined Services Forces, Armed Forces Reserve Command, Coast Guard Command, and Military Police Command.  Functionally, the GSH is in charge of formulating policies and supervising a wide range of military activities carried out by the armed services and other subordinate agencies, including joint war operations, political warfare, personnel, military intelligence, education and training, logistics, organization and equipment calibration, communications, military archives management, and medical services.[15]  It also plays a pivotal role in evaluating, coordinating, and overseeing force structure and related budgetary and equipment procurement decisions.  Overall, the GSH serves as the coordinating body and operational locus for

---

[12]The CGS would serve as both the military staff for the defense minister and commander of military operations under the defense minister's supervision. Hence, this revision in the National Defense Law would also expose the CGS to greater legislative oversight, as a leading official of the executive branch solely under the direct authority of the premier.

[13]During the legislative review process, the LY had expressed significant concerns regarding the draft National Defense Law and requested that further revisions be undertaken by the military.  As a result, Defense Minister Tang Fei ordered the military to produce a revised draft.

[14]The implications of placing what appears to be significant amounts of operational control over the military into the hands of an ostensibly civilian-led MND operating under the formal authority of the ROC premier (and not the ROC president) are far from clear, according to interviewees.

[15]*1998 National Defense Report, Republic of China*, p. 165; *The Republic of China Yearbook 1997*, p. 124.

the defense strategy/force structure and budgetary/procurement processes within Taiwan's defense policy arena.

The core[16] of the GSH consists of the chief of the general staff (CGS), the four vice chiefs of the general staff (VCGS) (who, together with the CGS, constitute the office of the chief of the general staff), and the five deputy chiefs of the general staff (DCGS) for planning (J-5), logistics (J-4), operations (J-3), intelligence (J-2), and personnel (J-1).[17] The VCGS includes one executive VCGS and three VCGS, each of the latter drawn from one of the three armed services. As indicated in Figure 2, each VCGS oversees one or more DCGS positions: VCGS/Navy oversees DCGS/intelligence, VCGS/Army oversees DCGS/planning and DCGS/operations, and VCGS/Air Force oversees DCGS/logistics and DCGS/personnel. The executive VCGS oversees the activities of all three VCGS posts.

The CGS is by far the most powerful and influential figure within the GSH. As the only four-star general rank officer within the GSH, he is the most senior active duty officer within the ROC military.[18] Under the current dual military authority system, the CGS acts, in the military command system, as chief of staff to the president for operational matters; in the administrative system, he serves as chief of staff to the minister of national defense.[19] Moreover, the relationship of the CGS to the four VCGSs is clearly one of a staff superior to line subordinates. This is because, unlike the U.S. military system, in which the members of the Joint Staff are the respective chiefs of each armed service, the four VCGSs of the ROC military are administrative

---

[16]As indicated in Figure 2, the GSH contains several offices which are not specifically discussed here because they do not play a critical role in influencing defense policy, force structure, budgetary, and procurement decisions.

[17]Under a ROC Military Organization and Force Restructuring Program (*guojun junshi zuzhi ji bingli tiaozheng guihua*, also known as the Streamlining and Consolidation (*Jing Shi*) Program) approved by Lee Teng-hui in December 1996, a J-6 office is to be created by June 2001 to handle communications and information warfare. This GSH office will be formed by merging the MND Bureau of Communication and Electronics and the Management Information Center under the J-5. It will be supervised by the VCGS/Navy. The Jing Shi Program is discussed in greater detail below.

[18]The executive VCGS is a so-called "first rank" three star; the VCGS are three stars (holding the same rank as service CinCs); and the DCGSs are two stars (holding the same rank as service deputy CinCs).

[19]*The Republic of China Yearbook 1997*, pp. 123–124.

figures separate (but equal in rank) to the service chiefs, and are appointed by the CGS. Their primary responsibility is to serve as the most senior professional advisors to the CGS and to generally support administratively the activities of the CGS as the most senior members of his staff.[20]  The executive VCGS coordinates the activities of the three VCGS offices, oversees the details of GSH activities on behalf of the CGS, and often acts in the latter's name and with his authority to handle some of the most important issues facing the GSH.  But he is clearly beholden to the CGS, as are the other three VCGSs.  The latter exist specifically to oversee the activities of the respective J1-5 offices for which they are responsible and to provide expert advice and support to the executive VCGS and CGS as needed.  They thus do not "represent" the interests of their services within the GSH.

The five DCGSs direct the activities of the individual J1-5 offices within the GSH.  Each of these offices is responsible for devising and overseeing the implementation of military-wide plans and activities in their respective functional areas, following the general guidelines contained in Taiwan's basic five-year and ten-year defense plans, using inputs provided by the individual services,[21] and under the coordination of the VCGSs.  Those offices exercising the greatest influence over planning and procurement decisions are J-5 (planning), and, to a lesser extent, J-4 (logistics).  The former takes primary responsibility for drawing up the military-wide defense plan, through input provided by the individual services and the other GSH offices.[22]  It also takes the lead in formulating military-wide procurement decisions, based upon the planning and related force structure parameters and procurement proposals developed under its supervision.[23]  The J-4 is primarily responsible for carrying out

---

[20]Moreover, the VCGSs perform their duties without the benefit of large staffs.  They generally rely, for administrative support, on the staffs of the J1-5 offices.

[21]Each service has its own office in charge of planning, logistics, operations, intelligence, and personnel issues.

[22]The J-5 performs staff analysis of specific service plans, usually in coordination with J-3 (operations) and J-2 (intelligence).

[23]One knowledgeable interviewee indicated that the J-3 (operations) office should logically take the lead in evaluating military equipment needs but that the J-5 does so because the ROC military depends heavily on foreign weapons purchases and the J-5 contains strong expertise on foreign weapons systems and their sources.

force structure and procurement decisions, i.e., it implements acquisition decisions, including contract negotiations.[24]

Despite its formal role as a broad coordination and supervision mechanism for the armed services, the GSH in reality serves more precisely as a staff agency for the CGS. This means that, on the one hand, the character, personal relations, and service orientation[25] of the CGS exert a significant, sometimes decisive, influence over the operations and outlook of the GSH. Each CGS is generally able to shape the general contours of Taiwan's defense policy and force structure in ways that potentially benefit the interests of his particular service. This is especially the case when an Army officer serves as CGS, given the historically privileged position enjoyed by the Army within the ROC armed forces and the continued high concentration of active and retired senior Army officers within the upper ranks of the GSH and the MND. On the other hand, because it does not contain the most-senior leaders of each armed service, the GSH cannot effectively and authoritatively coordinate the activities of the individual services. Although it certainly can enforce decisions upon the services, these decisions are those of the CGS, not those of the CGS *plus* the service chiefs (as in the case of the U.S. Joint Chiefs of Staff). The existence of the GSH as a separate leading bureaucratic entity from the armed services thus in the view of many observers presents a potential obstacle to the establishment of true jointness among the three services.[26]

A GSH Office of Defense and Strategic Studies (ODSS) (*Guofang Zhanlue Yanjiu Shih*) was established by General Tang Fei during his tenure as CGS to strengthen the ability of the GSH to undertake more coordinated and thorough strategic analysis of a range of critical security issues. Although the ODSS was formally established in December 1998 and its existence was publicly announced in March 1999, it has been informally operating under the direct supervision of

---

[24]However, the J-4's level of influence over the implementation of procurement decisions might be decreasing in favor of the MND Procurement Bureau, according to some interviewees.

[25]The post of CGS rotates among the three services, usually every two years.

[26]The Zhong Yuan Program of military reform (discussed below) would have greatly strengthened the operational link between the GSH and the combat units of the armed services. However, this element of the program has apparently been eliminated.

Tang Fei since at least 1996. Hence, although currently lodged within the GSH under the supervision of J-2, the ODSS might soon be relocated to the MND to facilitate Tang Fei's direct control over it and to strengthen the MND's overall capabilities in strategic analysis. The ODSS is currently undertaking strategic research and analysis in four major areas: ballistic and cruise missile defense, the revolution in military affairs (RMA), military confidence-building measures (CBMs) with the Mainland, and aspects of PLA modernization. The office is composed of several rising colonels and also receives input and analysis informally from a few civilians. For example, Professor Lin Zheng-yi of Academia Sinica is reportedly taking primary responsibility for CBM-related issues for ODSS and another civilian official is involved in RMA research.[27]

The effectiveness of the ODSS is not yet clear, however. It might suffer from two apparent drawbacks. First, despite the informal support it receives from a few outside civilian experts, the office is composed wholly of military officers, with current ROC statutes making the formal assignment of civilians to broaden this office difficult if not impossible. Second, the office is under the J-2 (deputy chief of staff for intelligence), almost certainly limiting its independence and effectiveness. Yet the ODSS has reportedly not lost its spirit and desire to bring some measure of badly needed rationality and reform to Taiwan's processes for developing strategy and acquiring the means to implement it.

## Armed Services General Headquarters

The General Headquarters for the ROC Army, Navy, and Air Force are directly subordinate to the GSH.[28] These offices are in charge of

---

[27]This use of civilian advisors in the defense sector was initiated by Tang Fei and overcomes years of military resistance to such a practice.

[28]Four other service general headquarters are also directly under the GSH but are not discussed because they do not play a significant role in the defense policy process. These are the Combined Services Force General Headquarters (in charge of ordnance, military maps, communication equipment, and the adoption of a joint logistic system for "general purpose" logistics for the ROC Armed Forces), the Armed Forces Reserve Command (in charge of reservist management and mobilization affairs), the Coast Guard Command (in charge of securing and protecting the coastline from intrusion and smuggling), and the Military Police Command (in charge of guarding specific military and government installations and serving as supplementary police when

"planning, force buildup, combat readiness, training, and logistics" for their respective service.[29] Each service headquarters is under the command of a commander-in-chief. Each CinC is a three-star general and is thus equal in rank to the three "ordinary" VCGS within the GSH. Each service CinC exercises clearly dominant authority over his service headquarters in a similar manner to that exercised by the CGS within the GSH. Each service headquarters also contains five core staff offices similar to the J1-5 offices of the GSH. For example, the Army General Headquarters contains the A-5 (planning), A-4 (logistics), A-3 (operations), A-2 (intelligence), and A-1 (personnel) offices. Hence, each service headquarters is in charge of developing and overseeing the formulation and implementation of that service's defense plans, force structure, and related budgetary and procurement proposals, within the larger national framework set by Taiwan's overall defense strategy and defense budget, under the supervision of the service CinC, and using the information and analysis provided by the service staff offices. As expected, each service headquarters thus acts as a strong advocate of its service's interests within the larger defense budget and procurement decisionmaking processes supervised by the GSH.

## Legislative Yuan

As stated in Chapter Two, the LY has become an increasingly important, independent actor in the national security arena in recent years. This development has been most clearly reflected in increased levels of LY scrutiny of the defense budget and equipment acquisitions by the LY National Defense and Budget Committees, and more frequent interrogations of defense and military officials before the LY National Defense and Foreign and Overseas Affairs Committees.

At present, no clear, dominant viewpoint on defense issues has emerged within the LY National Defense, Budget, or Foreign and Overseas Affairs Committees to replace the conservative viewpoints of pro-military KMT members. This is partly because opposition LY members have little expertise on defense-related issues and also

---

necessary). For further details, see *The Republic of China Yearbook 1997*, pp. 124–125 and the *1996 National Defense Report, Republic of China*, pp. 159–166.

[29]*1998 National Defense Report, Republic of China*, p. 165.

because the membership of the committees normally reflects a variety of views on national security and defense matters. The division between KMT and DPP members is at times especially sharp, with significant levels of mutual distrust in evidence.[30]

Many of those relatively few DPP members with views on defense matters believe that Taiwan's eventual independence can be assured only through (a) the possession of a *very* strong military capable of deterring China or, failing that, of blunting a Chinese attack and holding on for an appreciable period of time; and (b) Taiwan's formal participation in a regional security system led by the United States. For such DPP members, only the combination of these two elements will permit Taiwan to remain free from Chinese coercion and ultimately provide Taiwan with sufficient security to establish and maintain full independence from China.

For many DPP observers, the first step to attaining the above objectives is to bring the Taiwan military more fully under civilian control and to remove the dominant influence of conservative KMT elements over the military.[31] For such observers, the lack of adequate civilian oversight of the military and the dominant position within the officer corps enjoyed by conservative KMT elements together account for both the high levels of waste and the corruption that allegedly exist within the armed forces (purportedly involving sweetheart procurement deals between KMT officers and big business elements in the West and Taiwan) and the military's alleged continued resistance to adopting a more capable and appropriate defensive force structure containing fewer ground forces.[32] In

---

[30]The DPP still views the LY National Defense Committee as the "last bastion" of KMT conservatism in the political system, for example.

[31]The entrenched position of the KMT within the ROC military originates from the historical origins of the Nationalist military as an instrument of the Nationalist (KMT) Party. As Shambaugh points out (1996, p. 1292), both the KMT and the Chinese Communist Party "made great efforts to penetrate and control the armed forces with political commissars, and in both cases the armed forces have been more a political instrument of the ruling party than a government-controlled military." In the case of Taiwan, however, the KMT's grip on the military is clearly weakening as a result of the overall democratization process.

[32]Many DPP members believe that the Taiwan military places an excessive emphasis on the maintenance of inappropriate ground force capabilities, as opposed to more appropriate air and naval capabilities, because of the continued influence over the military of KMT Army officers.

addition, DPP observers believe that conservative KMT dominance of the military raises doubts about the loyalty of the military to a future non-KMT, independence-minded political leadership, given the strong opposition of many Mainlander KMT officers to the notion of Taiwan independence.

In countering these views, many KMT officers in the Taiwan military, as well as many conservative KMT politicians, argue that the DPP's primary intention in seeking greater legislative oversight of the military is to weaken the overall political strength of the KMT by eliminating its influence within the armed forces.[33]   They also fear that the DPP's efforts at military reform (including drastic reductions in the size of the ROC Army) will reduce Taiwan's aggregate military capabilities.

Although the above DPP views and the DPP-KMT confrontation over defense issues have yet to exert a major direct influence on Taiwan's defense policies, they have exerted a significant indirect influence by generating greater public support for closer media and LY scrutiny of the military, especially regarding defense strategy and budget/procurement matters—and especially in the wake of the procurement scandals of the early 1990s.  This development has produced four significant consequences to date.  First, and perhaps most notably, it has contributed to broader efforts by the LY to reduce defense spending in certain areas.  Such spending is increasingly seen as excessive because of corruption or as unduly benefiting the interests of KMT conservatives in the Army, as opposed to the overall interests of the military.[34]  Second, it has greatly extended the time required to complete the procurement process, as a result of greatly increased levels of LY involvement in that process.  Third, it has led to greater efforts by the MND to strengthen its role as an intermediary between the LY and the military.  The establishment in recent years of MND offices such as the Military Procurement Bureau was motivated in large part by the increased need to respond to LY

---

[33]Some KMT conservatives also undoubtedly believe that DPP views regarding the Taiwan military serve to assist Lee Teng-hui in his presumed efforts to reduce conservative KMT influence within the military.

[34]For example, DPP members frequently press for reductions in the procurement of Army equipment, under the assumption that such material is acquired in excessive amounts as a result of conservative Army influence over the procurement process.

involvement in the procurement process. Fourth, it has contributed greatly to the effort to end the existing dual military administrative and command authority systems and place the GSH (and hence the CGS) entirely under the MND and thus subject to greater LY scrutiny.

Although the level of LY influence over defense matters increased significantly during the mid 1990s, it reportedly declined somewhat by the end of the decade. This has resulted primarily from (a) the continued failure of DPP and other opposition political parties to develop significant defense-related expertise, (b) the lowering of concerns among opposition political leaders about the political influence exerted over the military by conservative KMT members, and (c) the gradual convergence of views on many defense matters between mainstream KMT and mainstream DPP politicians.[35] Nonetheless, many opposition (and some KMT) LY politicians remain frustrated by what they view as a lack of accountability of the armed forces. The ability of the LY to oversee military affairs, including defense and national security strategies, could increase significantly in the future once a proposed streamlining of Taiwan's military authority system goes into effect. Under these reforms, not only will the LY be able to examine military views and decisions more closely, but it will also likely have the authority to evaluate defense budget and procurement issues *before* critical decisions are made and thereby more extensively shape the size and composition of the defense budget. Under current law, the LY can only reduce the defense budget or redistribute existing budgetary allocations; it cannot increase the budget.

## Impending Organizational Changes

The above summary of the major organizations and leaders of the defense sector, combined with the conclusions presented in Chapter Two regarding the broader national security policy apparatus, indi-

---

[35]This has apparently occurred in response to both external strategic and domestic political factors. The increasing military threat from the Mainland, for example, has arguably prompted greater cooperation on defense matters among political parties. Moreover, some knowledgeable observers assert that Chen Shuibian, the leader of the mainstream DPP and a strong presidential contender, has greatly reduced his sharp criticism of the military to strengthen his support among moderate voters. This shift has allegedly served to reduce overall DPP criticism of the military.

cate that Taiwan's defense policy process is primarily centered within the professional military.  In particular, Taiwan's defense strategy and force structure are primarily determined by the GSH, within the broad parameters provided by Taiwan's overall national security policy, and with critical inputs from the service headquarters.  Civilian agencies, such as the MND and the president, perform general oversight and coordination functions, but neither is substantive at present.[36]  Moreover, this military-centered defense policy decisionmaking process is not well integrated into the civilian side of the national security policy process.  No formal institutions exist to provide ongoing and systematic policy formulation, implementation, and coordination of national-level grand strategies among civilian and defense policy sectors.  The NSC does not have the formal authority (or expertise) to perform this role, although it might acquire elements of such a role in the future.

In response to this deficiency, the National Defense Law contains a proposal to establish a National Military Council (NMC) (*guofang junshi huiyi*) as an authoritative, high-level defense decisionmaking organization.[37]  This body would be convened and chaired by the president and would include the vice president, premier, secretary-general of the president's office, NSC secretary-general, minister of national defense, chief of the general staff, and other individuals appointed by the president.  It would reportedly act as an ad hoc organization (i.e., with no permanent or fixed offices) and be convened by the president as part of his powers as commander-in-chief largely to make major decisions in the defense realm.  Less-important or less-urgent decisions would presumably be made by the president in private consultations with leading defense officials or possibly in the context of the above-mentioned military discussion meeting (*junshi huitan*), as is currently the case.

If organized as envisioned under the National Defense Law, the NMC would provide a means for bringing together the key members of

---

[36]Yet the level of influence over defense policy and procurement decisions exerted by individual senior civilian officials can vary significantly, depending upon the personal influence of the individual holding the office.  Taiwan's current highly competent and activist defense minister, Tang Fei, is reportedly increasing the level of MND influence over both decisionmaking arenas.

[37]Much of the following discussion of the NMC is based upon Ding and Huang (1998).

Taiwan's national security and defense leaderships to advise the president and make critical decisions. Presumably, such collective and authoritative participation in defense decisions would also strengthen overall policy coordination between the defense and foreign affairs policy realms. Yet the NMC essentially constitutes a more authoritative version of the senior leadership of the existing NSC, minus the minister of foreign affairs. Moreover, it would not have the in-house capacity to conduct policy analysis or evaluate the proposals submitted by key defense organs such as the MND or the GSH. Hence, despite its presumably greater authority, the effectiveness of the NMC would depend almost entirely upon the president's willingness to use the forum and the information and analysis provided by subordinate defense organs. Absent a highly proactive president in the defense arena, the uniformed military would thus likely retain its existing initiative and control over the defense policy process. Also, almost all interested legislators reportedly oppose the idea of establishing an NMC. Some argue that the NSC already performs the proposed functions of an NMC but simply needs to be made more authoritative and more subject to LY oversight.[38] As a result of such opposition, the NMC concept might be dropped, in favor of a stronger NSC.

Other organizational changes directly affecting existing defense organs were anticipated by extensive changes proposed when Admiral Liu Ho-chien served as CGS in the early 1990s.[39] The far-reaching Zhong Yuan (central field) Program developed at that time proposed several radical reorganization moves, including (a) dissolving the service general headquarters and dividing Taiwan into several unified commands directly under the CGS, (b) transforming the service CinCs into the VCGSs, (c) integrating the DCGS/planning (J-5) into the DCGS/operations (J-3), and (d) creating a new Operations Command directly under the CGS. However, these and other elements of the Zhong Yuan Program generated strong resistance among many

---

[38]At least one DPP legislator has proposed that the chairman of the NSC, i.e., the president, should be required by law to submit an annual report on national security strategy to the LY. See Ding and Huang (1998).

[39]The following two paragraphs are also based largely on Ding and Huang (1998).

senior ROC military officers, especially Army officers.[40]  As a result, the Zhong Yuan Program was essentially abandoned after Admiral Liu was replaced by Army General Lo Pen-li in mid 1995 and replaced by the less far-reaching but still significant Jing Shi Program.[41]

The Jing Shi Program, launched in mid 1997, focuses on streamlining higher-level command structures and consolidating lower-level troop units.  It is motivated by three basic requirements:  (a) the need to transition the ROC military from an offensive to a purely defensive stance, in response to the basic shift in ROC defense strategy outlined below; (b) the need to reduce organizational and procedural inefficiency and increase overall cost effectiveness and accountability, in response to budgetary pressures and growing public criticism of military corruption; and (c) the need to increase the flexibility, mobility, and general readiness of military units, in response to significant improvements in Chinese military capabilities.  The Jing Shi Program thus includes force cuts,[42] reductions in the size of the GSH,[43] reforms in military education and training, logistics reform,[44] and basic structural changes in military units, especially ground

---

[40]The ROC Army reportedly worried that "its share of the defense budget and its ability to shape military strategy would shrink substantially."  And service heads in general feared that the elimination of service general headquarters would excessively weaken the influence of each service and excessively reduce the number of senior officers leading each service.  Ding and Huang (1998), p. 10.

[41]The Zhong Yuan Program was closely associated with the ROC Military Ten-Year Force Target Program (*guojun shinianbingli mubiao guihua*), which was also superseded by the Jing Shi Program.

[42]The total manpower of the ROC military is to be reduced by more than 10 percent, from 453,000 to 400,000, and will include significant cuts in the size of the officer corps.  In addition, mobilization capabilities will be greatly improved.

[43]The total number of GSH personnel will be reduced by one-third of the 1997 level, and a new J-6 office (mentioned above) is to be established.  Major reductions in the size of the General Political Warfare Department (*zong zhengzhi zuozhan bu*) will also occur.

[44]Several military schools will be merged and the overall number of schools reduced from 30 to 20.  More important, professional training will be emphasized more and political indoctrination less.  A new Military Training Center (*guojia junshi xunlian zhongxin*) will be established to provide joint warfare training at the battalion level for all ROC units, and new doctrine development and training commands will be created.  Finally, logistics coordination among the three services will be strengthened.

force units.[45]  Those aspects of this program most relevant to force structure and procurement issues are discussed below.

## Defense Strategy and Force Structure Priorities

In the early 1990s, the ROC abolished its long-standing emphasis on retaking the Chinese Mainland and adopted in its place a national strategy keyed to peaceful coexistence, a nonviolent, democratically based reunification process, and an emphasis on the maintenance of Taiwan's domestic security and stability.[46]  As a result of this shift, Taiwan's military strategy now focuses entirely on the imperative of defending Taiwan's territory and population against coercive threats or direct attacks from the People's Republic of China.  Specifically, Taiwan's defense doctrine shifted from an emphasis on unified offersive-defensive operations (*gong shou yi ti*) to a purely defensive-oriented concept (*shoushi fangyu*), which excludes provocative or preemptive military actions against the Mainland.[47]  Of greatest concern to the ROC authorities are the threats to Taiwan's security posed by the possibility of air or missile displays or attacks, naval harassment or blockades, and amphibious and air-based invasions of territory under ROC control, including Taiwan, the Pescadores, Kinmen Matsu, and other smaller islands.[48]

For defense planners, Taiwan's primary military objective is to deter such PRC military threats and, if deterrence fails, to counter or repel PRC attacking forces and to maximize the survivability and sustainability of its own forces.  This objective presents enormous chal-

---

[45]Most notably, the ROC Army will gradually transition from a division-centered force to a combined arms brigade-centered force.  The above core components of the Jing Shi Program are described in greater detail in Ding and Huang (1998).

[46]In 1991, President Lee Teng-hui terminated the "Period of Mobilization against Communist Rebellion" and abolished the "Temporary Law of Mobilization and Suppression of the National Rebellion."

[47]Huang (1997), pp. 282–283.

[48] These three basic sets of military threats can take a variety of forms, including the conduct of military exercises that simulate attacks against Taiwan, ballistic missile attacks intended to panic the Taiwan populace or paralyze the ROC military's air defense and C3I systems, limited or extensive naval interdiction efforts, the mining of ports, and large-scale assaults against Taiwan's offshore islands or the Taiwan Mainland.

lenges, largely because (a) China is a very large potential adversary possessing significant resources, (b) the main island of Taiwan is located less than 100 n mi from China, and (c) Taiwan is a long, narrow island offering little opportunity for maneuver and defense-in-depth. On the other hand, Taiwan's situation also presents some significant defense-related advantages. Its considerable economic strength permits the maintenance of a relatively robust military force and the acquisition of quite sophisticated weapons platforms and support systems, albeit in relatively small numbers and often subject to the availability of foreign suppliers.[49] Moreover, despite the proximity of Taiwan's main island to the Chinese Mainland, the Taiwan Strait separating the two sides presents a serious challenge to any effort by Beijing to successfully deploy forces capable of destroying Taiwan's major military assets and seizing and holding Taiwan's most critical population centers. Assuming that the morale of the Taiwan populace and its military would remain firm in the face of Mainland air and naval attacks or blockades, such an effort would likely require a large-scale amphibious assault across nearly 100 n mi of often rough seas. At present, the Chinese military lacks the extensive amphibious warfare experience, training, and equipment that would make such an assault possible. In addition, the approaches to the western coastline of the island of Taiwan (i.e., the side facing the Mainland) are dominated by very wide mud flats and offer very few good invasion landing sites. Thus, the overall challenge posed to Mainland Chinese defense planners when contemplating the military conquest of Taiwan are by no means insignificant, despite Taiwan's strategic vulnerabilities.

Taiwan's defense policy is thus guided by two strategic concepts: resolute defense (*fangwei gushou*) and effective deterrence (*youxiao hezu*). The former concept is largely political and connotes the determination of the Taiwan military to defend all the areas under its control without giving up any territory. The latter concept connotes

---

[49]At present, the main forces of the ROC military consist of an army of approximately 250,000 combatants and support personnel (centered on ten infantry divisions and two mechanized infantry divisions), two divisions of marines, 700+ main battle tanks, 36 principal naval surface combatants (destroyers and frigates), 53 missile patrol boats, 500+ combat aircraft (with ongoing delivery of 60 Mirage 2000-5 and 150 F-16 A/B), 31 naval combat aircraft, and 21 armed naval helicopters. For details, see *The Military Balance 1998/1999* (1998), pp. 197–198.

the commitment to building and maintaining a military capability sufficient to severely punish any threatening or attacking force and to deny such a force the attainment of its objectives.[50]

To accomplish these defensive tasks, however, and given its above-mentioned vulnerabilities (in particular, its relative lack of strategic depth), the Taiwan military must be able to conduct significant off-shore operations in the event of a serious threat from China. Hence, Taiwan's defense planners employ a four-layer defense-in-depth strategy that places a high priority on three types of military capabilities. The four layers of Taiwan's defense include (1) a front line that encompasses the defense of ROC territory in close proximity to the Chinese Mainland, including the highly fortified islands of Quemoy and Matsu; (2) the middle line of the Taiwan Strait, which has served for over 40 years as an unofficial but mutually understood "boundary" separating PRC and ROC air and naval forces; (3) Taiwan's coastline, which must be successfully defended to ensure the defeat of any invasion force; and (4) the western plain of Taiwan, which must be successfully defended to prevent any invading forces from securing Taiwan's north-south Chongshan Highway and thereby gaining rapid access to the entire island.[51]

To implement this four-layer, defense-in-depth strategy, Taiwan's military forces must be able to succeed in carrying out three key missions, listed in general order of priority: (1) air superiority (*zhikong*) for the ROC Air Force, (2) sea denial (*zhihai*) for the ROC Navy, and (3) anti-landing warfare (*fandenglu*) for the ROC Army.[52] Each mission is generally viewed by each service as constituting a relatively separate and distinct task. In other words, Taiwan's defense strategy is not based upon the concept of joint warfighting. This is reportedly due in part to the small size of the ROC military, the limited expanse of the battlespaces involved, the limited technical capabilities of Taiwan's weapons systems, and the purely defen-

---

[50]Huang (1997), pp. 284–285.

[51]Huang (1997), pp. 286–288.

[52]The first two missions reportedly enjoy the highest priority, given the importance of air and sea denial capabilities to preventing air or missile attacks, blockades, and invasions and the fact that Beijing is currently stressing the improvement of its air and naval power projection capabilities.

sive nature of the mission given to each service.[53] It also reflects the severe restrictions on operational capabilities imposed by Taiwan's relatively small defense budget, which does not permit even the most basic, individual mission of each service to be fully implemented.[54] More broadly, the separate warfighting missions of each military service reflect the larger "stovepiped" nature of the ROC military structure as a whole.[55]

In recent years, however, a greater emphasis has been placed on developing joint operations capabilities. The creation of joint air-sea-land missions was reportedly originally included under point (a) of the above-mentioned Zhong Yuan Program supported by former CGS Admiral Liu Ho-chien, i.e., as an integral part of the establishment of regional unified commands under the direct command of the CGS. Under this plan, Taiwan's armed forces were to be reorganized to defend two defense zones (the small islands of Quemoy and Matsu) and four operations zones (Northern, Central, Southern, and Eastern Taiwan). Air, ground, and naval forces within each of these zones were expected to independently conduct joint operations.[56] This "operations zone" concept was not formally included in the subsequent Jing Shi Program. However, it reportedly remains popular among younger officers, as does the concept of jointness in gen-

---

[53]According to one ROC military interviewee, "The United States places a great emphasis on joint warfighting because such a capability is critical for success when large numbers of forces are deployed in offensive operations across large areas. In contrast, the ROC's relatively small forces must carry out a purely defensive mission in a very small area."

[54]Taiwan's defense budget was slightly more than $10 billion in 1997, whereas the PRC defense budget is generally estimated by most well-informed analysts as somewhere in the range of $30 billion to $35 billion. Moreover, because of the increasing cost of social welfare programs and infrastructure investment, the share of Taiwan's defense budget as a percentage of both total government expenditures and GDP has fallen in recent years. And much of Taiwan's defense budget is taken up by huge personnel costs, which greatly exceed both operational costs and military purchases. In the FY99 defense budget, these three categories of expenditure accounted for 50.5 percent, 19.09 percent, and 30.86 percent, respectively. Moreover, arms acquisitions represent only a very small portion of overall military purchases. See Ding and Huang (1998), pp. 2–3.

[55]As indicated above, the relative lack of operational and policy coordination among the three armed services is confirmed by the absence of any direct link between the leadership of the GSH and the leadership of the service headquarters.

[56]Huang (1997), p. 289.

era⌐, despite the continued separate influence exerted over defense planning by the individual services. Moreover, efforts to develop joint operations have made some significant headway in the areas of C3I and EW/reconnaissance, where jointness is becoming increasingly necessary.

Officially, the concepts of "resolute defense" and "effective deterrence" suggest that Taiwan must acquire the capability to carry out the above three military missions successfully without outside assistance. In reality, however, ROC defense planners realize that Taiwan is almost certainly incapable of effectively resisting an all-out and prolonged attack from the PRC without help from the United States. Therefore, Taiwan's defense strategy is primarily designed, on the operational level, to hold out and give the United States ample time to intervene. This effort consists of two basic components: First, to deflect or slow down a PRC attack, primarily by blunting the PRC air campaign and disrupting Chinese naval deployments in the early stages of an attack by deploying a limited number of forces in a sharp ccunterattack[57] (this counterattack will consist primarily of determined efforts to intercept and destroy attacking Chinese air and naval forces);[58] and second, to retain adequate reserves of air, naval, and land forces; withdrawn to the eastern side of Taiwan supposedly beyond the range of many PRC weapons, to preserve Taiwan's ability to defend itself while awaiting U.S. assistance. Specifically, such reserves can continue to harass PRC attacks piecemeal, to challenge a prolonged blockade or invasion, and to show the United States that Taiwan still retains a viable defensive force worthy of being rescued. ROC forces reportedly hope to be able to survive with this strategy for a *maximum* of 90 days.

The weakest link in Taiwan's four-layer defense-in-depth strategy is obviously the first link: defense of the offshore islands. Although protected by approximately 50,000 troops, these islands are well

---

[57]The ROC Air Force plans to remain viable during this initial stage of combat for a minimum of 15 days.

[58]Such actions might also include attacks against Chinese air and naval bases on the Mainland, especially if Taipei were to conclude that Beijing had launched an all-out effort to subdue the ROC. However, to our knowledge, major, concerted counterstrikes against Mainland-based military assets do not constitute an integral part of Taiwan's defense strategy.

within artillery range of Mainland forces and would almost certainly prove unable to withstand a major Chinese invasion (as opposed to a sustained long-range artillery or missile barrage). Moreover, the islands could probably be by-passed with little difficulty in the event of a major attack on the main Taiwan island, thus neutralizing their military benefit to Taipei. As a result of these considerations, it is very likely that the ROC leadership does not regard the defense of the offshore islands as absolutely critical to the success of its overall security strategy and would thus probably not commit significant resources to their preservation, especially in the event of a major Chinese assault against Taiwan. In contrast, Taipei might expend considerable resources in the defense of the islands if Beijing opted to apply only limited military pressure against them as part of a coercive diplomatic strategy, given their value as symbols of Taiwan's determination to resist Chinese aggression and their potential utility as a possible tripwire for U.S. intervention.[59] Indeed, an attack on the offshore islands could very well prompt some type of U.S. response.

The above defense strategy (and in particular the three core missions of the ROC armed services) has certain clear implications for Taiwan's required force structure. In general, the strategy posits a relatively narrow and separate view of each service's equipment needs, although such narrowness has been declining in recent years as efforts are made to develop a modest level of joint warfighting capability, noted above.

The ROC Air Force's main air superiority mission is to destroy whatever PLA Air Force assets are deployed against Taiwan. In other words, air-to-air interception takes priority over other possible missions. Hence, the ROC Air Force places a high priority on upgrading its combat aircraft and strengthening reconnaissance and early warning systems and on acquiring advanced medium-range air-to-air missiles. In recent years, largely in response to the need to improve joint warfighting capabilities, the ROC Air Force has been

---

[59]During the Chiang Kai-shek and Chiang Ching-guo eras, the offshore islands also had considerable symbolic value as tangible indicators of the Republic of China's political claim to all of China, given their close geographical proximity to the Mainland. However, such value has arguably declined greatly, in the minds of many observers, since the Lee Teng-hui government relinquished its claim to the Mainland in 1991.

gradually developing both air-to-ground and air-to-sea attack capabilities.  Hence, it is striving to increase its arsenal of weapons such as the Harpoon and the Maverick missiles.  Yet the ROC Air Force is still viewed as being too small and underfunded to fill full-fledged ground- and sea-support roles in addition to its primary air intercept mission.[60]  In addition, efforts to develop more robust air-to-surface capabilities are limited by the fact that the ROC military believes that the U.S. Department of Defense resists providing Taiwan with such capabilities because it fears that they could be employed for offensive purposes, against ground or sea targets on or near the Chinese Mainland.

One additional priority area for ROC Air Force modernization is early warning and air defense.  Taiwan has no integrated EW/air defense system, in part because the ROC Army and Air Force have not agreed to integrate their respective capabilities.  Moreover, many of Taiwan's land-based air defense early warning and C3I installations are highly vulnerable to sabotage or missile strikes, reportedly because the ROC Army will not provide adequate troops to protect airfields and ports.  Hence, the ROC Air Force is exerting greater efforts to improve its EW and air defense capabilities and reduce the vulnerability of its air defense facilities to a sudden attack. This effort received increased support from the GSH after ROC Air Force General Tang Fei became CGS in February 1998.  General Tang will no doubt continue to support these developments as defense minister.

The ROC Navy insists that the greatest threat to Taiwan is posed by a combination of a naval blockade and a small but steady number of missile attacks against unpopulated targets, intended to panic the Taiwan populace, demoralize the ROC military, and hence eventually force the ROC to accept reunification largely on Beijing's terms.  The ROC Navy's sea denial mission thus focuses almost exclusively on countering various forms of Chinese naval blockades.  Of greatest concern to the ROC Navy is the threat posed by China's large number of submarines and the recent and ongoing qualitative improvements in the capabilities of China's surface and subsurface combatants.  Thus, Taiwan's naval modernization programs stress improvements in shipboard electronic and combat systems, ship-to-

---

[60]Huang (1997), p. 288.

ship missiles, and antisubmarine warfare (ASW) capabilities. The ROC Navy's ASW and mine warfare capabilities have been significantly upgraded in recent years through the acquisition of new surface combatants and mine hunters.[61] Nonetheless, the ROC Navy wants to acquire still more advanced surface platforms. To fight in the Taiwan Strait, air and missile defenses would also be required. The ROC Navy thus seeks systems including Aegis-equipped ships with the Standard Missile-2 (SM-2) and long-range detection and anticruise missile capabilities. Moreover, senior naval officers and strategists believe (somewhat illogically given the slow speeds and resultant low search rates of these vessels) that advanced diesel submarines constitute the best platform for both ASW and strategic deterrence and continue to press foreign suppliers for such a platform.[62] The ROC Navy also desires long-range P-3 Orion maritime patrol aircraft, claiming that the S-2T airborne antisubmarine aircraft now being provided by the United States do not have the range and endurance required to remain on station for extended periods of time in a crisis. In general the ROC Navy does not focus on acquiring combat aircraft capabilities because it believes it is still greatly deficient in performing its primary antiblockade mission and because a robust naval air arm could produce major coordination and communications problems with the ROC Air Force. The ROC Navy focuses its air and missile defense efforts on obtaining improved surface-to-air missile systems.[63]

The ROC Army reportedly believes that the most likely Chinese military threat is a sudden, rapid attack against the Taiwan Mainland.

---

[61]Huang (1997), p. 288.

[62]Huang (1997), p. 288. The latter point was confirmed by the author in numerous interviews conducted with ROC military personnel. Many foreign observers believe that the ROC military seeks advanced submarines to conduct preemptive mining and attack operations against Chinese ports and warships, to quickly reduce the ability of the PLA Navy to deploy its large number of naval vessels against Taiwan in a crisis. The United States has denied the ROC request for advanced conventional submarines, claiming that they are inherently unsuited to ASW operations and, more important, are offensive weapons and hence not included in the category of "defensive" weaponry permitted under the Taiwan Relations Act.

[63]Even such missile systems would pose potential coordination and communication problems with the ROC Air Force. The general problem of potential "friendly fire" contacts between ROC naval and air forces in a major conflict with the Mainland highlights the need for a joint operational doctrine and capabilities on and over the Taiwan Strait. I am indebted to Paul Godwin for this observation.

Such an attack would have three coordinated elements: (1) the seizure of Taiwan's main ports by a small number of paratroop units; (2) the severe disruption of Taiwan's power, early warning and C3I installations via combined ballistic missile attacks and sabotage conducted by PRC fifth column elements (believed by the ROC Army to total as many as 30,000 individuals); and (3) the landing of an invasion force at Taiwan's ports, to be conveyed by an armada of commercial and military vessels of various sizes. For the ROC Army, the most threatening elements of the PLA's arsenal thus consist of its ground forces (including its commando/airborne attack units), its fifth column elements, and its ballistic missiles. Hence, the ROC Army's antilanding warfare mission is primarily directed toward countering paratroop attacks, followed by a large-scale amphibious assault on Taiwan.

The transition from the Army's original mission of retaking the Mainland to the present mission of defending ROC territory against a Chinese assault, combined with the need to respond to improvements in Chinese ground force capabilities (especially the establishment of rapid reaction units and improvements in airborne operations capabilities), has required a basic shift in the ROC Army's force structure. On the one hand, the Army's modernization program stresses improvements in existing weapons systems such as heavy artillery, land-based antiship and surface-to-air missiles, helicopters, and main battle tanks such as the M-48H and M60A3. At the same time, the ROC Army is attempting to increase the mobility, flexibility, and responsiveness of its combat units by creating combined arms brigades (*lianhe bingzhong lyu*). This new brigade-based force will include five types of units: infantry brigades, armored infantry brigades, tank brigades, special operations brigades, and air cavalry brigades. Thus far, the composition of only two types of brigades has been revealed. Armored infantry brigades (*zhuangbu lyu*) are being formed to counter airborne paratroop invasion and for rapid response, whereas airborne cavalry brigades (*kongqi lyu*) are being created to repulse armored attacks, control riots, defend against an airborne paratroop attack, and serve as a strategic reserve unit. These forces will require advanced combat helicopters, as well as light armored vehicles of various types.[64]   The Army is reportedly establishing experimental formations at the battalion and brigade level for all five types of brigades and plans to operationalize all five brigades by 2000.   Together, the above five brigades will constitute main striking brigades (*dajilyu*), which will be supported by second-line defense infantry brigades (*shoubeilyu*).[65]

The above overview of the ROC military's primary mission and its implications for the force structure of the three armed services suggest an array of current and future equipment needs, from more sophisticated and integrated C3I and reconnaissance and early warning systems, to more advanced surface combatants, more advanced air-to-air and air-to-surface missiles, submarines, improved ASW platforms, and more capable countermeasures against ballistic missiles.   In addition, as the Jing Shi Program clearly indicates, the ROC military will also need to undertake a costly streamlining, restructuring, reeducating, and retraining of its administrative and combat units to create the kind of force that the ROC believes will be capable of meeting the Chinese threat over the long term.   Despite such a considerable array of hardware and software service needs, budgetary and manpower limitations, technical constraints, leadership preferences, and the hesitancy of most foreign suppliers to provide specific weapons systems together place significant limits on what and how much Taiwan can acquire and absorb, especially over the near to medium term.[66]   All of these factors, and others, must be

---

[64]Ding and Huang (1998), p. 13. The armored infantry brigade will be equipped with M-41 tanks, M-113 armored personnel carriers, M-48H main battle tanks, and M-109 artillery.   The airborne cavalry brigade, administered by the newly formed Army Airborne Special Operations Command, will be equipped with AH-1s, OH-58s, UH-1Hs, and B-23s—all helicopters.   Despite its recent emphasis on mobility and rapid response, the Army reportedly continues to acquire heavier armored vehicles such as the M-60 tank.   This acquisition is reportedly viewed as a stopgap measure—to provide for continued defensive capabilities against light armored attack until larger numbers of more-mobile antitank platforms (including combat helicopters) can be acquired.

[65]Ding and Huang (1998), p. 13.

[66]Specific additional limiting factors not mentioned above include (1) the corrosive effects on warfighting capabilities produced by Taiwan's two-year conscription system, which undermines the development of adequate skill levels, especially in the Navy and Air Force; and (2) a host of internal personal, political, and cultural obstacles within the ROC military that limit its capabilities.   These obstacles include an excessive reliance on officers, in place of a career noncommissioned officer corps, a lack of

considered and resolved or mitigated through the procurement process.

## THE WEAPONS PROCUREMENT DECISIONMAKING PROCESS

According to interviewees, before the procurement scandals of the early 1990s, the procurement decisionmaking process tended to be extremely secret, limited to a few participants, quite irregular, and highly influenced by personal relationships and interests. Since the scandals, the process has become more regularized, more attuned to the operational requirements and preferences of the services, but also much more lengthy and complex.

The procurement decisionmaking process includes the following seven basic elements. Although listed in general order of execution, these elements do not always follow one another in sequence; i.e., some elements overlap or even coincide with one another.

- The establishment of ten-year, five-year, and annual defense plans and budget levels by the DCGS/J-5, under the oversight of the MND, and following guidelines set by Taiwan's overall defense strategy and force restructuring programs.

- The development of a set of military-wide procurement proposals by the DCGS/J-5, based upon requests submitted by the individual services.

- The evaluation and, if necessary, revision, of service-wide procurement proposals by the CGS and their submission to the MND for comment and assessment.

- The approval of the military's major procurement decisions by the president and the premier.

- The investigation of specific procurement items by the LY.

- The discussion with U.S. authorities of specific weapons systems or support systems desired from the United States.

---

lower-level problem-solving and initiative, and a poor level of officer recognition of the need for sophisticated information warfare (IW) and battle management systems.

- The implementation of specific procurement decisions by the MND Procurement Bureau, under the supervision of the DCGS/J-4 office.

## Defense Plan and Budget Determination

This element of the procurement process establishes the basic force structure and budget guidelines for determining specific procurement proposals and decisions. ROC defense plans and budgets have been determined since 1975 loosely on the basis of the well-known Planning, Programming, and Budgeting System (PPBS) originally developed by the U.S. Department of Defense under former Defense Secretary Robert McNamara.  This system seeks to closely integrate and coordinate the basic features of Taiwan's force structure plan (including ten-year, five-year, and one-year force modernization, restructuring, and readiness plans) with concrete long-term, mid-term, and annual financial requirement programs and specific long-term, mid-term, and annual defense budget plans.  The basic parameters for the entire PPBS process are established by Taiwan's overall defense strategy and service missions (outlined above) and the general annual, five-year, and ten-year national budget estimates set by the Executive Yuan and examined and authorized by the Legislative Yuan.  The final product of the PPBS process is the military budget.

Both force structure and subsequent defense budget plans are developed by the DCGS/J-5, using input (in the form of data and proposals) provided by the planning offices of the individual service headquarters.  This process is supervised and coordinated by the VCGS/Army[67] and, if necessary, the executive VCGS.  In general, the defense plans submitted by the services must adhere to or reflect the specific mission of each service.  Moreover, the long-term (i.e., ten-year) defense and budget plans normally provide basic guidance for the five-year and annual plans.  Annual force structure and budget plans (and especially the latter) generally roll over from year to year on the basis of these longer-term plans and hence contain few major changes.  However, both plans can sometimes fluctuate significantly,

---

[67]The VCGS/Army does not represent Army interests in performing this task.  He is essentially a senior staff member for the CGS.

primarily because of changes in the perceived threat posed by the Mainland, the changing preferences of key decisionmakers such as the CGS, and the opportunities presented by the sudden availability of previously unobtainable foreign weapons. The latter two factors are of particular significance.

As part of his extensive influence over the operations of the GSH, the CGS has the authority to shape and alter defense plans and budget distributions to the individual services. These actions, in turn, can greatly influence subsequent procurement decisions. However, such influence consists primarily of shifts in the relative emphasis placed upon the forces or finances of a particular service, not wholesale transformations that fundamentally contravene the parameters set by long-term defense and budget plans.

ROC force modernization is highly dependent upon foreign supplies of major weapons platforms and support systems, especially given the significant shortcomings of Taiwan's indigenous defense industry.[68] However, most foreign suppliers are prevented or constrained from providing such equipment to the ROC because of strong Chinese opposition. Hence, when a previously denied system becomes available, Taiwan's military and political leadership will usually allocate the required funds.[69] This often creates a situation aptly characterized as "procurement directed planning and budgeting."[70]

Once the overall defense budget (including specific weapons procurement budgets) is determined by the professional military through the PPBS process, it is then evaluated by the MND before submission to the Executive Yuan/premier for final acceptance by the executive branch, and to the Legislative Yuan for approval. However, neither the MND nor the Executive Yuan normally possess the expertise to challenge specific elements of the defense budget and hence rarely reject or significantly modify the military's budget pro-

---

[68]Shambaugh (1996), p. 1302 discusses these shortcomings.

[69]Portions of the national defense budget are specifically allocated to indigenous and foreign weapons procurement, and  considerable extra budgetary funds are set aside annually for the purchase of certain high-priority foreign weapons systems. However, "breakthrough" purchase opportunities result in even larger special appropriations, often covering several years. See Shambaugh (1996), pp. 1296–1297.

[70]Huang (1997), p. 290.

posals. According to interviewees, both organs are primarily concerned with the implications of the budget for military-LY relations.[71] The LY possesses even less expertise to evaluate defense budget proposals. Nonetheless, that body has played a more interventionist role regarding both budget and procurement decisions. In the former area, the major effect of the LY thus far has been to press for reductions in the procurement budget, various parts of which are regarded as excessive because of corruption or as unduly benefiting the interests of KMT conservatives in the Army, as opposed to the overall interests of the military.

## General Procurement Proposal Formulation

This element of the overall procurement decisionmaking process is reportedly the most sensitive and secretive, given the sharp rivalry among the three services over acquisitions, the intense interest in individual procurement decisions exhibited by potential foreign (especially U.S.) suppliers and the U.S. Congress, and the acute sensitivity to Taiwan's foreign force acquisitions evinced by the PRC. The military's annual procurement proposal is formulated within the GSH by a military procurement committee directed by the DCGS/J-5, under the general supervision of the VCGS/Army, and on the basis of proposals submitted by the relevant service planning departments.

The members of the GSH procurement committee normally include all five DCGS/J1-5, the deputy CinCs of the three services (representing the interests of the service CinCs), and the senior staff members of the GSH/J-5 office (including officers loaned from the planning staffs of the three services). The committee meetings are usually convened and chaired by the DCGS/J-5. However, the VCGS/Army (a three-star) will chair the meetings when the service CinCs (also three-stars) are present. The latter will attend procurement meetings when agreement among the services becomes especially difficult.

---

[71]Again, this could change significantly under new Defense Minister Tang Fei. Tang is likely to take a much more active interest in details of the defense budget than did his predecessor.

The services individually determine their indigenous and overseas procurement priorities *and sources*[72] using a committee-based process similar to that of the GSH. Any desired systems costing less than New Taiwan (NT) $50 million can be procured independently by each service, but those systems costing more than NT$50 million must be submitted to the GSH procurement committee for formal approval. The individual services usually submit several procurement options to the GSH procurement committee in a given year, knowing that not all requests will be approved. Each year, budgetary and other considerations usually limit each service's procurement proposal to only two or three major weapons or support systems, along with a larger number of smaller requests.

Before the convening of the full procurement committee, the DCGS/J-5 consults with the other DCGSs/J1-4 to roughly prioritize the items requested for that year by each service; lower-priority items are usually reconsidered the following year. This assessment is based primarily on the perceived relevancy of each item to Taiwan's overall defense strategy and force modernization plan and its likely cost within the estimated defense budget for that year. The latter evaluation is generally guided by a desire to avoid items that take up significant portions of the entire defense budget, unless they are specifically (and strongly) favored by the CGS. The former evaluation consists largely of determining the relevancy of each service's request to its core defense mission. If the services submit requests for systems that directly support these core missions, they are more likely to be approved. As a result, the ROC Air Force will almost always stress the acquisition of capabilities directly relating to air-to-air interception, the Navy will almost always stress the acquisition of antishipping capabilities, and the Army will almost always stress the acquisition of equipment to oppose paratroop or amphibious landings on Taiwan.

Once the services' procurement requests are roughly prioritized, the full procurement committee meets to determine the formal military-wide procurement proposal to be submitted to the CGS and MND.

---

[72]It is important that each service determine the likely supplier for each desired weapons or support system, given the difficulties Taiwan faces in this area and the fact that, according to interviewees, any funding allocated for a particular system is forfeited if a supplier cannot be found.

These meetings are convened over a period of approximately three months, from September to December. They can at times be quite contentious and normally witness considerable "horse trading" of various systems. External influence on this process is also sometimes exerted by civilians such as the president and LY politicians. However, the most urgent items requested by each service are usually approved.

## CGS/MND Evaluation

All formal proposals for procurement items, whether determined by the GSH/J-5-led procurement committee or the individual services, must be submitted to the CGS. The CGS evaluates these proposals and can make changes before they are finalized and then submitted to the MND. The CGS can, and often does, press to obtain disproportionately high procurement orders for systems needed by his particular service.[73] However, such favoritism is not boundless or always in evidence. For example, conservative Army General Hao Pocun reportedly strongly supported greatly increased levels of spending for naval and air systems during his tenure as CGS. Each CGS must be attentive to the overall force structure requirements contained in the ROC's five- and ten-year defense plans.

The MND normally does not possess the expertise to evaluate or challenge specific procurement requests from a technical or operational perspective. However, the current defense minister, as an experienced former senior military officer, will probably query individual requests, as his predecessor did. Yet, as with Chiang Chung-ling, Tang Fei might only rarely, if ever, press to significantly revise the military's procurement proposal, given the longstanding dominance of the armed services over the procurement process.

---

[73]For example, Admiral Liu Ho-chien pressed for procurement items and a program of military restructuring (the Zhong Yuan Program) that arguably benefited naval and air forces, whereas the Army's interests tended to benefit when Army General Lo Ben-li served as CGS.

## President/Premier Evaluation

Both the president and premier must formally provide final approval for all procurement requests for systems in excess of NT$50 million, which are submitted to the GSH procurement committee for evaluation.  In reality, the premier almost invariably follows the lead of the president on such matters and hence does not play an influential role in the approval process.  Moreover, the president reportedly personally examines and approves the procurement of all items costing several million U.S. dollars.  Yet President Lee Teng-hui lacks the expertise (both personally and within his staff) to evaluate the technical/operational value or necessity of a requested system.  Thus, he usually relies on the views of the defense minister and the CGS when evaluating a particular procurement request.

Yet Lee has at times attempted to exert independent influence over procurement decisions.  According to one very knowledgeable military interviewee, the president's office sometimes seeks, during meetings of the procurement committee, to ensure the inclusion of one or two high-profile weapons systems at the expense of other less-prominent but equally important systems.  This is allegedly done, as noted in Chapter Two, because Lee Teng-hui generally views weaponry as symbols of reassurance and resolve, not as key components of a larger force structure designed to attain genuine warfighting objectives, and because he values U.S.-supplied weapons systems in particular as critical indicators of greater U.S. support for Taiwan.  Also, Lee's view on procurement issues might be influenced by more personal associations.  The brother of his Chief aide-de-camp, Rear Admiral Hsu Chu-sheng, is reportedly a major arms sale broker; hence some observers believe that Hsu influences Lee's assessment of procurement proposals on behalf of his brother.

It is extremely difficult to assess the extent to which presidential preferences influence the procurement decisionmaking process.  On balance, it seems that Lee Teng-hui's influence is highly sporadic and usually exerted in support of weapons systems that were already under serious consideration by the professional military, or at least significant parts of the military, on the basis of their merit as components of existing force structure modernization plans.  No interviewee stated that presidential intervention has resulted in the inclusion of weapons systems that were strongly opposed by the majority of the senior military leadership. Indeed, some interviewees insisted that the professional military is usually able to resist efforts by any civilian ROC official, including the president, to insert major procurement items into the budget contrary to their wishes.

## LY Intervention

The LY exerts even less influence over specific acquisition decisions than it does over planning and budget issues. No institutionalized or regularized process of legislative examination or supervision of the procurement process currently exists. In general, scrutiny of procurement proposals by the Legislative Yuan is sporadic and largely nontechnical, given its limited expertise on defense matters and its lack of access to the early stages of the procurement decisionmaking process.[74] The LY can request a hearing or a report on specific procurement items that it discovers or that are brought to its attention. However, the dominant influence over defense issues exerted by conservative KMT members on the LY National Defense Committee reportedly continues to prevent the LY from undertaking concrete or substantive changes in the procurement proposals prepared by the military and approved by the president and the Executive Yuan. Nonetheless, LY-induced decreases in the defense budget have at times resulted in reductions in the number of items procured in a given year by the military. In addition, the increased involvement of the LY in all facets of the procurement decisionmaking process has greatly lengthened the time required to complete the procurement process.[75]

## U.S./ROC Discussions

Several ROC interviewees insist that the most significant type of influence exerted by non-ROC military participants over the procurement decisionmaking process originates from the United States.

---

[74]However, if the CGS is formally placed solely under the MND in the military authority system, the LY will then have the formal authority to inquire about procurement decisions before such decisions are made.

[75]Some interviewees assert that the greatly increased time required to obtain LY approval of the government's procurement proposals sometimes results in the collapse of preliminary negotiations with suppliers.

U.S. influence over Taiwan's procurement decisionmaking process derives primarily from two distinct sets of interactions between ROC and U.S. representatives:  (1) meetings between U.S. Department of Defense or diplomatic officials and ROC representatives or military officers concerning specific defensive military systems, and (2) unofficial interactions between U.S. politicians and private businessmen and ROC government officials and politicians concerning specific procurement orders.

The former set of interactions includes both informal ad hoc meetings during the early stages of the procurement process, at which ROC officials inform U.S. officials which military systems Taiwan will likely request from the United States in a given year, and formal annual meetings at which U.S. officials inform ROC officials which military systems the United States is willing to provide in a given year.  These interactions provide the ROC with a clear sense of the sort of military systems the United States is willing to provide and hence establish general guidelines for many procurement decisions.[76]   However, ROC officials are only authoritatively informed of U.S. decisions to provide specific systems at the annual ROC-U.S. meeting, which is usually held after the ROC government finalizes its procurement decisions.  Hence, this mode of U.S. influence over the ROC procurement process is limited.

The latter set of interactions reportedly exerts a greater level of influence over ROC procurement decisions.  Many U.S. Congresspersons have a very strong interest in Taiwan security issues, for both national security and pro-democracy reasons, and in response to the narrower political and economic interests of their constituencies.  In addition, many U.S. defense industries have an obvious interest in expanding their level of business with Taiwan through increased U.S. military sales to the island.  As a result, U.S. political representatives and businesses will often take an active interest in the type and origin of various weapons systems available to Taiwan and will at times

---

[76]The number of such interactions has increased in recent years, as part of an overall expansion in the level of contact between the U.S. and ROC militaries resulting from the March 1996 Taiwan Strait "mini-crisis." That event, which involved the deployment of U.S. naval forces to the vicinity of Taiwan, brought to light the extent to which U.S. forces lack adequate communication with and understanding of the ROC military.

express their preferences regarding such systems to ROC officials, including both high- and low-level individuals responsible for defense policy and procurement issues. This is particularly true of U.S. corporations with very active representative offices in Taipei; they have much easier, and more direct, access to ROC defense officials. Local representatives of major U.S. defense industry corporations often urge that the specific military-related systems they manufacture be included in the annual procurement proposals prepared by the GSH. In addition, such industry representatives have also reportedly at times attempted (thus far without success) to convince LY members to pass procurement laws beneficial to their interests. In general, this type of informal and indirect U.S. involvement has frequently influenced the procurement process, according to knowledgeable observers.[77]

## Implementation

The decision to proceed with contract negotiations and purchase decisions for military systems is made by the DCGS/J-5 once the ROC government finalizes its procurement proposals for the year and discussions have been held with U.S. authorities regarding those systems the United States is willing to provide to Taipei. The DCGS/J-4 oversees and coordinates the implementation process, which is formally carried out by the MND Procurement Bureau.

## Overall Assessment

Despite the dominant role in the procurement decisionmaking process played by the professional military and the increasing regularization of that process, those who deal with the ROC military—both U.S. and other knowledgeable observers on Taiwan—view the procurement system as frequently driven by considerations other than careful strategic analysis. Individual services continue to set priorities, sometimes on the basis of traditional bureaucratic rivalries or even personal considerations, rather than on rigorous

---

[77]For example, according to at least one informed observer, it resulted in a decision to purchase U.S.-made Stinger surface-to-air missiles rather than the French Mistral missile, even though the latter was reportedly preferred by many in the ROC military.

analysis of overall warfighting needs based on an integrated threat-centered defense strategy.[78]   Many observers also suspect that Taiwan's military and political leadership too often decide to acquire a major weapons platform largely because it has been approved for sale by foreign suppliers (so-called "availability-led procurement"). This process has at times apparently been responsible for often disjointed, but conspicuous, additions to the ROC arsenal.  There is at least a realization now among some senior military officers, almost certainly including Minister of Defense Tang Fei, that a more rigorous process—one that more closely follows the actual U.S. PPBS approach (or a scaled-down version of that elaborate scheme)—should be seriously considered for Taiwan.

Finally, many observers of Taiwan's procurement process believe that the ultimate utility of any weapons system acquired by the ROC is greatly hampered by the failure of the ROC military to fully assimilate and maintain its more advanced weapons.  For a variety of reasons (e.g., excessive emphasis on the political symbolism of major weapons systems, inadequate funding, the failure to develop a mid-level career NCO corps, service rivalries, and short-term enlistment rates), many observers believe that the ROC military pays inadequate attention to proper maintenance, resupply, crew training, and coordinated operations training among the forces of the three services.

---

[78]A hypothetical example, based on a real issue for Taiwan's defense, may help illustrate this issue.  Taiwan is legitimately concerned about the threat from the PRC's large and improving submarine force—composed of modern as well as other diesel-electric and nuclear-powered attack submarines.  However, it appears to many that Taipei has looked at the problem in a somewhat cursory way and decided it needs submarines of its own and greatly improved antisubmarine aircraft to replace its S-2Ts.  Taipei, it seems to the critics, should analyze more fully the nature of the submarine threat to its interests and focus on coping with that threat, even if it concludes that the threat cannot be effectively dealt with by any means but looking to American ASW to intervene.  Such a conclusion need not mean that nothing would be procured. Deterrent ASW forces well short of those required to win in a head-to-head conflict may actually be quite useful, if recognized in the overall strategy for what they are.  I am grateful to Eric McVadon for providing this illustration.

# Chapter Four

# CONCLUSIONS AND POLICY IMPLICATIONS

The analysis in this report suggests several answers to the questions presented in the introduction concerning the power structure, policy process, and underlying concepts governing ROC decisions on national security, defense policy, and procurement issues. These answers, in turn, have implications for U.S. policy toward Taiwan, especially in the areas of arms sales and the broader U.S. defense relationship with the ROC military.

Taiwan's national security policy process (i.e., the formulation and implementation of ROC national strategic objectives and the major principles guiding both foreign and defense policies) is concentrated in the hands of a few senior civilian and military leaders and at times strongly influenced by the views and personality of the president. Moreover, this process is poorly coordinated, both within the top levels of the senior leadership and between the civilian and military elite. As a result, the ROC at present lacks a comprehensive, explicit national security strategy that can integrate and guide Taiwan's foreign and defense policies. Of particular note, Lee Teng-hui's initiatives in the foreign policy realm do not appear to be either conceptually or operationally coordinated with a larger national security strategy. Similarly, ROC defense policy is largely determined by the senior leadership of the ROC military almost entirely on the basis of a relatively narrow military defense plan. It does not appear to flow from or support the objectives of either a broader national security strategy or of Taiwan's foreign policy as presently conceived. This overall lack of strategic coordination sometimes leads outside observers to suspect that Taiwan's foreign and defense policies are largely determined by the political or personal objectives of individual senior leaders, especially the president.

Taiwan's defense strategy and defense policy process provide the foundation for a relatively narrow set of service missions and force structure requirements keyed primarily to the separate interests and outlooks of the three services and an assumption of U.S. intervention in a future major military confrontation with the Mainland. Few organizational, financial, or conceptual incentives exist to promote more comprehensive and integrated approaches to defense planning that systematically and consistently link perceived threats to doctrine, force structure, training, and maintenance needs. Moreover, evidence suggests that advanced weapons systems are sometimes desired and/or acquired from foreign sources without full consideration of the appropriate operational and maintenance requirements of such systems. Indeed, procurement decisions are at times significantly influenced by a host of factors other than pure warfighting needs, including the political objectives of the president. This results in considerable confusion over the motives behind Taiwan's individual weapons procurement decisions and resulting foreign purchase requests and a lack of confidence among many outside observers in the ability of the ROC military to gain the maximum benefit from the more advanced weapons systems it acquires from the United States and elsewhere.

The above general conclusions have implications for the U.S. defense relationship with Taiwan, especially regarding the sale of military equipment.

First, the United States should continue to acquire more and better information on the overall strengths and weaknesses of Taiwan's national security strategy, defense doctrine, and procurement decisionmaking process. This is necessary both to assist the ROC in rationalizing its defense planning and budgeting process and to more accurately assess Taiwan's requests for military sales from and cooperation with the United States. It is especially critical for the United States to avoid providing arms and assistance to Taiwan that serve to strengthen the U.S.-ROC defense relationship in ways that provoke greater tension with the Mainland without appreciably improving Taiwan's defense capabilities in areas deemed critical by the United States. The United States should thus continue to strengthen and expand its defense-related contacts with the ROC in ways that serve the above ends.  This should include strategic dialogues and advice and assistance designed to improve equipment training, procurement and acquisition processes, and management techniques.  At the same time, the United States should exercise utmost caution with respect to interactions with the ROC that might be construed as aimed at the establishment of joint operational capabilities (i.e., so-called interoperability) between ROC and U.S. combat forces, such as procedures for coordinating air and naval deployments in a crisis.  Such actions arguably violate existing U.S. limits on the type of assistance that can be provided to Taiwan under the Taiwan Relations Act[1] and could give China the impression that the United States regards Taiwan as a security partner.  Such a misperception could significantly damage Sino-U.S. relations and prompt Beijing to deploy military forces against Taiwan.

Second, the United States should strive to develop and maintain close contacts with and knowledge about Taiwan's key national se-curity and defense decisionmakers, especially the president, minister of defense, NSC secretary-general, and chief of the general staff.  The personalities and views of these individuals exert a major influence over critical defense-related decisions.  It is extremely important for the United States to understand who these individuals are and how they relate to one another and the larger national security and de-fense policy apparatus.  The improvement of contacts with such leaders could be carried out in ways that do not excessively provoke the Mainland Chinese government.

Third, the United States should be aware that a variety of motives could lie behind each of Taiwan's requests for major weapons sys-tems and types of security assistance and that some systems and their operators might not receive adequate training and support ser-vices.  Although at least some segments of the military usually strongly support every such request, attempts should be made to

---

[1]Section 3 of the Taiwan Relations Act stipulates that "the United States will make available to Taiwan such defense articles and defense services in such quantity as may be necessary to enable Taiwan to maintain a sufficient self-defense capability." This statement has been consistently interpreted to mean that the United States may pro-vide articles and services to Taiwan for use in its self-defense but does not imply that the United States can or should establish a joint defense capability with Taiwan.

identify and disentangle military from possible nonmilitary motives and to realistically assess (and convey to the ROC government) what is required to deploy and maintain a particular major weapons system. The United States should also work with the ROC to reduce the influence of parochial U.S. political and business interests on ROC arms purchase requests.

Bates, Gill, "Chinese Military Hardware and Technology Acquisitions of Concern to Taiwan," in James R. Lilley and Chuck Downs, eds., *Crisis in the Taiwan Strait*, National Defense University Press, Ft. McNair, Washington, D.C., September 1997.

Bitzinger, Richard A., "Military Spending and Foreign Military Acquisitions by the PRC and Taiwan," in James R. Lilley and Chuck Downs, eds., *Crisis in the Taiwan Strait*, National Defense University Press, Ft. McNair, Washington, D.C., September 1997.

Cheng Hsiao-shih, *Party-Military Relations in the PRC and Taiwan: Paradoxes of Control*, Westview Press, Boulder, 1990.

Ding, Arthur Shufan, and Alexander Chieh-cheng Huang, "Taiwan's Military in the 21st Century," a paper prepared for the Eighth PLA Conference, Aspen Institute, Wye Plantation, Maryland, September 11–13, 1998.

Dreyer, June Teufel, "A History of Cross-Strait Interchange," in James R. Lilley and Chuck Downs, eds., *Crisis in the Taiwan Strait*, National Defense University Press, Ft. McNair, Washington, D.C., September 1997.

Huang, Alexander Chieh-cheng, "Taiwan's View of the Military Balance and the Challenge It Presents," in James R. Lilley and Chuck Downs, eds., *Crisis in the Taiwan Strait*, National Defense University Press, Ft. McNair, Washington, D.C., September 1997.

Jencks, Harlan W., "Wild Speculations on the Military Balance in the Taiwan Straits," in James R. Lilley and Chuck Downs, eds., *Crisis in the Taiwan Strait,* National Defense University Press, Ft. McNair, Washington, D.C., September 1997.

*The Military Balance 1998/1999,* The International Institute for Strategic Studies, Oxford University Press, London, October 1998.

Nien-dzu Yang, Andrew, "Taiwan's Defensive Capacities," in Greg Austin, ed., *Missile Diplomacy and Taiwan's Future: Innovations in Politics and Military Power,* Strategic and Defence Studies Centre, Research School of Pacific and Asian Studies, Australian National University, Canberra, 1997.

*1996 National Defense Report, Republic of China,* Li Ming Cultural Enterprise Co., Ltd., Taipei, 1996.

*1998 National Defense Report, Republic of China,* Li Ming Cultural Enterprise Co., Ltd., Taipei, 1998.

*The Republic of China Yearbook,* Government Information Office, Republic of China, 1997.

*The Republic of China Yearbook,* Government Information Office, Republic of China, 1998.

Shambaugh, David, "Taiwan's Security:  Maintaining Deterrence Amid Political Accountability," *The China Quarterly,* No. 148, December 1996, London.

Yang, Andrew N. D., "Taiwan's Defense Buildup in the 1990s: Remodeling the Fortress," in Gary Klintworth, ed., *Taiwan in the Asia-Pacific in the 1990s,* Allen and Unwin, St. Leonards, Australia, 1994, pp. 71–88.